WARTIME MEMORIES

WARTIME MEMORIES

STORIES OF WORLD WAR II
AT HOME AND ON THE FRONT

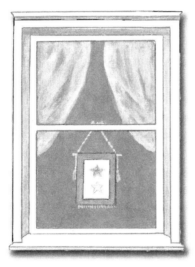

BY THE RESIDENTS OF RIVERMEAD
PETERBOROUGH, NEW HAMPSHIRE

Cover painting by RiverMead resident Gay Hartman

All photographs are courtesy of the authors and their families

Published by the RiverMead Residents' Council in collaboration with
Yeoman House Books, Tiverton, Rhode Island 02878

Copyright © 2012 RiverMead Residents' Council and the authors

All rights reserved. No part of this book may be reproduced in any form or by
any electronic or mechanical means, including storage and retreival systems,
without permission in writing from the publisher, except for the purposes of a
published review which may quote brief passages in such a review. Anyone who
would like to obtain permission for reproduction of any of the material in this
book should contact:
  RiverMead
  Attn: Wartime Memories
  150 RiverMead Road
  Peterborough, New Hampshire 03458

Printed in the United States of America

ISBN: 978-0-9852537-0-7

This is a paperback edition published simultaneously with the hardcover version
of this title, ISBN: 978-0-9822659-9-4

Contents

Foreword viii
Acknowledgements ix
Timeline of World War II events x

Part One: The European Theater

Map of the European Theater 18
Fighting With the 7th Armored Division,
   William C. Arthur 19
Creating the Harbor at LeHavre, Theodore S. Bacon 24
The 106th Station Hospital,
   Jeanne McCutcheon Britton 26
Displaced Persons in Bonn, Robert S. Fellows 30
The War Seen From Britain, Thomas H. Forman 36
Spy Games After the War, Sym Goodnow 39
Gathering Storm, Louise Guion 41
The Convoys of Sierra Leone, René Isaac 43
A Witness at Buchenwald, Robert D. Johnson 47
The Invasion of Normandy, John M. Keefe 52
The 10th Mountain Division in Italy, F.O. Lathrop 60
The Deserted Village, Bruce McClellan 62
Adventure in the Bay of Biscay, Dr. Glyn Millard 66
Denmark Under German Occupation, Birgit Faber Morse 68
The War from Beirut, Peter Oliver 73
A Gentle Voice on the Battlefield, G. Blake Sabine 77
On the Ground with the Third Armored Division,
   Philip A. Stoddard 81

From Flight Training to Radio Repair,
   Richard Swahnberg 87
The War From Berlin, Karin Van Strien 90
Letters to the Homefront, Roger B. Wilson.................................... 99
The War in Photos, Europe ***111***

Part Two: The Pacific Theater

Map of the Pacific Theater 115
The 70-Ton Crane That Sent Us Home,
   Sheppard Bartlett 116
From the Coast Guard to Korea, David Clinkenbeard 119
The Irony of War, John Goodhue 128
The Combat Piano Player, Peter Hewitt 130
From Convoys to Weather, Carl B. Jacobs 132
The Right Place at the Right Time, Andrew Kordalewski........... 134
Destroyer Duty in the North Atlantic and South Pacific,
   Doug Maynard... 136
View from the Bridge: The Marshall Islands Invasions,
   Harold C. Moore Jr. 139
The Day We Hit the Mine, Win Nelson 151
Tough Duty, Donald M. Sherk 153
"Wonders" in the Pacific, Cal Sholl... 155
A Ticket to See the World, Arthur L. Stevenson........................... 160
The War in Photos, Pacific ***162***

Part Three: The Home Front

The Victory Garden, George L. Andersen 166
Our Lives Would Never Be the Same, Bailey Arthur 173
Memories, Marcie Blauner... 176
My Friend Nobie, Mileva Brown 177
Navy Corpsman in Training, George F. Cahill Jr., M.D...............179
A Surgeon is Born, Robert A. Chase, M.D. 180

Spies in Connecticut, Barbara Clark 183
Life at the Norfolk Naval Base, Judith E. Collier 184
Dear Dad, Warner B. Cornwall 186
Snapshots of War, Julie Crocker, M.D. 188
The Inverted Spin, James Faller 191
When the War Bonds Paid Off, Sharon H. Goldsmith 193
Uncle Bob Missing in Action, Molly Goodnow 197
Engineering and Expediting, Polly Gottschalk 199
The Little Nite Club, Susanne Holcombe 200
South Meets North, Christine S. Kelly 201
My Special Day, Augusta Foster Law, M.D. 203
Moving Around with the "FlyBoys,"
   Helen W. Livingston 205
No Ordinary Time, Mary Elizabeth McClellan 208
The Lighting Designer, Robert W. McKinley 211
Meeting That Special One, Irene Peacock Moore 213
Sheltered from the Storm, Edith V. Parker 218
Uranium and Spies, Margo Potter 219
Boot Camp in the Bronx, Hazel S. Quick 221
Helping with the JANGOS, Evelyn Schmitt 227
Bumped, Nan Sholl 229
Actors on the Deck, Sidney A. Walker 232
Defending Fishers Island, Alan Wilder 233
The Warrior from Pan Am, John J. Young 239
The War in Photos, The Home Front ***246***

List of Contributors 247

Foreword

Behind Those Windows

During World War II, it was a common sight – little red and white flags with blue or gold stars displayed in front windows all across our country. The blue star indicating a family member serving in the military – a gold star honoring a member lost in combat.

Whether or not adorned by a flag, stories of courage and sacrifice were played out behind those windows. Civilians as well as service personnel learned to cope and sacrifice during those challenging times.

Residents of RiverMead, a retirement community, reflect on the life of a nation joined in a world at war. Some of the experiences deal with tragedies of battle. Others, with humility and humor provide a counterpoint to the realities of war. All deal with the common goal of preserving our freedom. It was everyone's war.

This book is not intended as anything more than a documentary of the life and times of a group of men and women sharing their own experiences. However, in reflecting on the past, it is natural to ponder the present and the future. In an era of continuing global conflict, hopefully the lessons of history will contribute to future tales of peace and prosperity for all nations.

Acknowledgements

The Wartime Memories Project

This book of Wartime Memories came to life under the guidance and leadership of Mary Elizabeth McClellan, president of the RiverMead Residents' Council. Having seen two similar books, it sparked the idea of producing one at RiverMead. She assembled a coordinating committee consisting of Charlotte Goodhue, Gay Hartman and Cal Sholl to explore the idea. The results of a residents' survey were positive and the project came to life.

The stories are from many sources and all are related to a RiverMead resident in some way. Several are posthumous, others written long ago when the memories were fresh. Most were composed for the book and were either dictated, retyped from hand written notes or composed on the computer. This work involved several residents, especially Chris Brown, Molly Goodnow, Rick Hartman, Sally Pore and Rosie Wilson who typed, interviewed, transcribed and proofread. Charlotte Goodhue was tireless in tracking down period and recent photos of all the authors. Cal Sholl wrote our Foreword inspired by Gay Hartman's cover design.

We thank Bonnie Cohen, CEO, and Jan Eaton, Director of Resident Services & Marketing, for their encouragement and RiverMead's financial support. We also thank Sherry Gauthier, Executive Assistant, who worked with us and the publisher to smooth the transfer of all the material and photos. Her computer and organizational skills saved us lots of time and frustration.

We hope you enjoy this collection of amazing accounts from amazing people who lived in a challenging time in our history.

Timeline of World War II

Pre-War

1921 *July 29:* Adolph Hitler becomes leader of the National Socialist (Nazi) Party
1922 *October 28:* Benito Mussolini becomes head of the Italian government
1923 *November 8:* Hitler and other Nazis jailed after failed attempt at a government takeover in Munich's "Beer Hall Putsch"
1925 *July 18:* Publication of Hitler's *Mein Kampf* (My Struggle)
1929 *October 29:* Stock market crashes on Wall Street
1930 *September 14:* In German elections, Nazis become second-largest political party
1931 *September 18:* Japanese troops invade and occupy Manchuria
1932 *November 8:* Franklin Delano Roosevelt elected President of the United States
1933 *January 30:* German President von Hindenburg names Hitler Chancellor of Germany
1934 *June 30:* "Night of the Long Knives" a violent purge of the leadership of Germany's SA Storm Troopers who had threatened Hitler's power
August 19: Hitler declares himself Fuhrer
October: "Long March" of Chinese Communists led by Mao Zedong begins
1935 *March 16:* Despite dictates of the Versailles Treaty, Germany begins military conscription
September 15: Nuremburg Race Laws enacted, stripping German Jews of citizenship and most civil rights
October 3: Italian forces invade Ethiopia
1936 *February 10:* The Gestapo, under Heinrich Himmler, assumes absolute control over internal German security
March 7: German troops reoccupy the Rhineland in violation of the Versailles Treaty
May 9: Italy annexes Ethiopia

July 17: Civil War begins in Spain, with Fascist General Franco leading the "Nationalists" against the "Loyalists"
November 1: Roosevelt reelected as President of the United States
November 6: Germany sends planes and pilots to Spain to support the Nationalists
November 26: Anti-Comintern Pact signed by Germany and Japan

1937 *January 19:* Japan officially withdraws from 1921 Treaty limiting size of its navy
April 27: Spanish city of Guernica destroyed by German air attack
May 28: Neville Chamberlain succeeds Stanley Baldwin as British Prime Minister
June 11: Soviet purge of Red Army officers begins
July 31: After beginning hostilities with China, Japan occupies Beijing
September 19: Japanese launch air raids on Nanking and Canton
November 8: Japanese take over Shanghai, killing 100,000 Chinese troops and 200,000 civilians
December 13: Nanking falls to Japanese army; "Rape of Nanking" kills some 200,000 civilians

1938 *January 28:* Roosevelt calls for massive rearmament program for U.S.
March 12: Germany announces Anschluss (union) with Austria
March 13: New Nazi government in Vienna declares Austria a province of the German Reich
September 30: Hitler and Chamberlain meet in Munich, agree to cede Czechoslovakia's Sudetenland to Germany, which Chamberlain claims will bring "peace for our time."
October 1: German troops occupy the Sudetenland
November 4: Japan declares Nine Powers Treaty of 1922, which guaranteed China's independence, as obsolete
November 9: The Kristallnacht pogrom ("Night of Broken Glass") unleashes widespread attacks on German Jews.

The War Years

1939 *January 26:* Spanish Nationalists seize Barcelona
February 27: France and Great Britain recognize Franco's government in Spain
March 15: Nazi troops occupy all of Czechoslovakia
March 28: Nationalists declare victory in Spanish war
May 1: Germany begins gassing executions of mentally and physically disabled
May 22: Hitler signs Pact of Steel treaty with Mussolini
August: Germany and the U.S.S.R. sign a non-aggression pact
September 1: German forces invade Poland; Britain and France declare war; United States proclaims its neutrality
October 9: Hitler issues orders for invasion plan of France and the Low Countries
October 14: German U-Boat sinks *HMS Royal Oak* at anchor in Scapa Flow, killing 883.
November 30: Soviet Union invades Finland, Winter War begins

1940 *January 8:* Rationing of butter, sugar and bacon begins in Britain
March 12: Finland signs peace treaty with the Soviet Union
May 9: Germany invades Denmark and Norway
May 10: Germany invades Holland, Belgium and Luxembourg
May 10: Chamberlain resigns as British Prime Minister; Winston Churchill is asked to form new government
May 13: Churchill makes his "blood, sweat, tears and toil" speech in House of Commons
May 26: Operation Dynamo, the evacuation of British, French and Belgian troops from Dunkirk begins; Belgium formally surrenders on the 28th
June 10: Italy declares war on Britain and France
June 14: German troops enter Paris
July 1: French government of Marshal Petain established in Vichy

July 10: German air forces begin the Battle of Britain
July 23: Soviet Union officially obsorbs Lithuania, Latvia and Estonia
August 23: German air raids on central London begin
August 25: First Royal Air Force air raid on Berlin
September 13: Italian forces invade Egypt
September 16: U.S. enacts peacetime draft law
October 7: German troops enter Romania
October 28: Italy invades Greece

1941 *January 22:* Tobruk, Libya falls to British and Commonwealth troops
February 12: General Rommel and the Afrika Korps arrive in Tripoli
March 11: Roosevelt signs the Lend-Lease Act
April 27: German troops occupy Athens, Greece
June 22: Germany launches Operation Barbarossa, the massive invasion of the Soviet Union
July 26: U.S. freezes Japanese assets in the U.S. and suspends diplomatic relations
August 14: Churchill and Roosevelt sign the Atlantic Charter
September 3: First gassings of prisoners at Auschwitz begins
September 9: German's 900-day siege of Leningrad begins
September 19: German forces take Kiev and 600,000 Soviet prisoners
October 2: German army launches operation on Moscow
December 7: Japanese naval and air forces attack U.S. naval base at Pearl Harbor, Hawaii
December 8: U.S.A. declares war on Japan; Britain and Commonwealth do same
December 10: Japan begins invasion of the Phillipines

1942 *January 5:* Tire rationing begins in the U.S.
January 16: Japan invades Burma
February 1: Germany begins mass deportations of Jews from Western Europe to extermination camps in Poland

February 15: British surrender to Japanese forces at Singapore

February 19: Roosevelt issues executive order authoring the internment of Japanese-American citizens

February 27: Allied naval forces heavily damaged in Battle of Java Sea

March 8: Japanese forces capture Rangoon; Dutch East Indies surrenders the next day

May 4-8: battle of the Coral Sea

May 15: U.S. begins gasoline rationing

May 30: Royal Air Force launches 1,000-bomber raid on Cologne

June 4-7: U.S. wins decisive Battle of Midway, sinking four Japanese aircraft carriers

July 1-27: Battle of El Alamein in North Africa

August 8: U.S. Marines take Henderson Field on Guadalcanal

October 23: Second Battle of El Alamein begins

November 4: German troops begin retreat from El Alamein

November 8: Operation Torch: U.S. invasion of North Africa

1943 *January 10*: Soviet Army begins offensive against Germans in Stalingrad

January 18: Jews in Warsaw ghetto begin uprising against Nazis

January 23: U.S. troops take Tripoli

February 1: Field Marshall Paulus surrenders to Soviets in Stalingrad

Februrary 14: Battle of Kasserine Pass in Tunisia begins

March 16: Climax of the Battle of the Atlantic: 27 merchant ships sunk by German U-boats in one week

May 7: Allies take Tunis

July 9: Allied invasion of Sicily (Operation Husky) begins

July 25: Mussolini is arrested by order of the Italian King, ending the Fascist regime

September 8: Italy surrenders unconditionally to Allies; German forces rushed to Italy

September 9: Allies land at Salerno and Taranto
September 12: Mussolini rescued by German paratroopers
October 13: Italy declares war on Germany
November 1: U.S. Marines land in Solomon Islands
November 20: Marines land in the Gilbert Islands
November 28: Roosevelt, Churchill and Stalin meet at the Teheran Conference
December 12: Rommel takes over as commander in chief of French coastal defenses for Germany
December 24: Eisenhower appointed Supreme Allied Commander, Europe; Montgomery, C-in-C of the 21st Army Group

1944
January 17: Allies attack Germans at Cassino, Italy
January 22: U.S. Fifth Army lands at Anzio, 30 miles south of Rome
January 27: Siege of Leningrad lifted after 900 days, 1 million casualties
February 1: U.S. troops begin fight for Kwajalein in the Marshall Islands
March 4: Allies launch first daylight air raid on Berlin
May 9: Soviets recapture Sevastopol
May 18: Allies capture Italian town of Monte Cassino
May 26: Charles DeGaulle proclaims his Free French movement to be the provisional government of the French Republic
June 4: Allies enter Rome, first Axis capital to be liberated
June 6: D-Day (Operation Overlord): Allies invade Normandy, France
July 4: Allies have landed some 920,000 troops in France, with more than 62,000 men killed, wounded and missing
July 21: Marines land on Guam
August 8: U.S. completes capture of Marianas Islands
August 15: Allies launch Operation Dragoon, invasion of southern France
September 3: British Second Army liberates Brussels
September 17: Allies launch Operation Market Garden,

with airborne troops parachuting into Eindhoven, Nijegen and Arnhem to secure bridgeheads.
September 25: British rescue remaining paratroopers from Arnhem: just 2,163 survivors from original 10,000.
October 14: Implicated in plot against Hitler, Rommel commits suicide
October 20: U.S. begins invasion of Leyte, Phillipines; three-day naval Battle of Leyte Gulf rages from the 23rd.
November 18: U.S. Third Army crosses the German frontier
December 16: Germans launch fierce counterattack, "The Battle of the Bulge" in the Ardennes
December 21: Germans besiege U.S. paratroopers in Bastogne, capture St. Vith
December 26: Bastogne relieved by U.S. 4th Armoured Division

1945 *January 9:* U.S. troops land on Luzon, the Phillipines
January 17: Soviet troops capture Warsaw
February 4: Roosevelt, Churchill and Stalin meet at Yalta
February 14: German city of Dresden is firebombed by Allies, killing more than 40,000 civilians
February 19: U.S. Marines begin amphibious assault on Iwo Jima; the famous flag-raising takes place on the 23rd
March 7: U.S. troops cross the Rhine River at Remagen
March 9: B-29 bombing creates firestorm in Tokyo, destroying 16 square miles and killing more than 100,000 civilians
April 1: U.S. troops land on Okinawa
April 12: U.S. President Franklin Roosevelt dies in Warm Springs, Ga.
April 30: Hitler commits suicide in his bunker in Berlin
May 7: German General Jodl signs Germany's unconditional surrender
May 8: V-E Day (Victory-in-Europe Day) proclaimed
June 5: Allies divide Germany in four Zones of Occupation
June 18: President Harry Truman authorizes "Olympic," an invasion plan for Japan scheduled to begin in November
July 16: First U.S. atomic bomb is successfully tested at

Alamogordo, N.M.

July 26: Clement Attlee is elected Prime Minister of Great Britain, replacing Churchill.

August 6: U.S. drops atomic bomb on Japanese city of Hiroshima, killing some 140,000 people.

August 8: Soviet Union declares war on Japan and invades Manchuria

August 9: U.S. drops second atomic bomb on Nagasaki, killing some 80,000 people.

August 14: Japan surrenders

September 2: Japanese sign surrender agreement aboard *U.S.S. Missouri* in Tokyo Bay, officially ending the war

Information courtesy of the National WWII Museum, New Orleans, La.

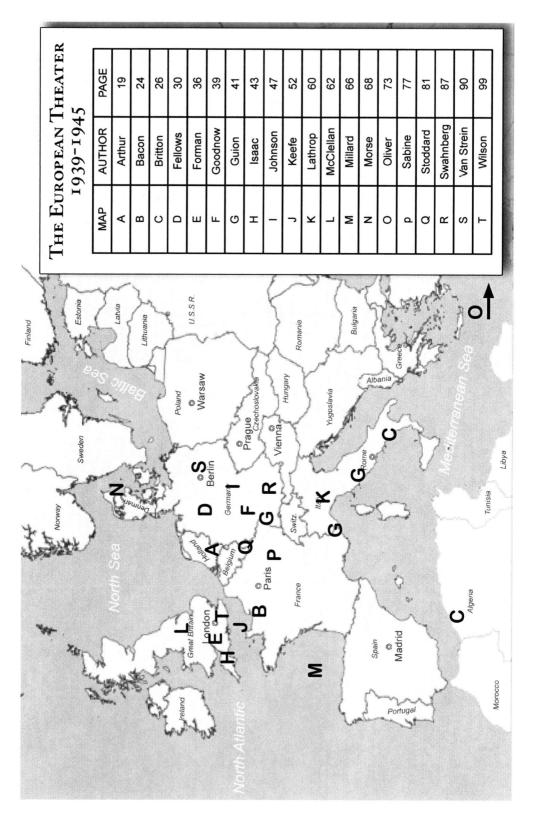

PART ONE
The European Theater
FIGHTING WITH THE 7TH ARMORED DIVISION

WILLIAM C. ARTHUR

In November of 1943, my unit was loaded onto a train at Camp Kilmer [New Jersey] with all the blinds pulled. We were taken to the Hudson River where the cars were loaded onto a barge and taken to a transport ship in a convoy headed for Europe. The *Monarch of Bermuda* was flat-bottomed and rode pretty rough. There were 120 ships and 8 troop transports in the convoy around the U.S.S. *Texas* with a top speed of 12 knots. The convoy broke up two weeks later near the coast of England. Our ship went to Liverpool where the units that had been below were let off first. That was only right as our unit had been on the promenade deck with plenty of fresh air and sunshine and not much seasickness.

In England, my unit, A Battery, 953rd Field Artillery, was put onto a railroad car which was dark and, again, had the shades pulled. We traveled all night not having any idea where we were going. We finally stopped and were allowed out and marched to a little village called Thorverton in Devonshire. The locals were very friendly. We quickly found the local pub where we ordered Scotch but only got British beer.

Our unit stayed on maneuvers near by, and it got pretty boring. I discovered an opportunity to apply for a job at SHAEF headquarters in London and went up and tried but was turned down. The young major there said, "Well, you have a weekend pass, why don't you stay and have some fun?" I remembered Colonel Gregory, who had been the superintendent of Culver Military Academy, was stationed there, so I looked him up and found out that he was nearby in Bryanston Square. I went looking for him and located him in a temporary office working on a bunch of orange crates. I knocked, and the Colonel said, "Who's there?" I replied, "Lieutenant Arthur, Sir." And he said, "Arthur, where the hell have you been? I've been looking for you. I know what Culver men can do, and there are about 25 of you over here and I want you transferred up here now! I've got thirty days to staff this office." He invited me to dinner at the Royal Automobile Club.

At dinner he explained his plan for the Culver men. He wanted to transfer me to the 12th U. S. Army Group headquarters in London. With instructions to keep mum, I returned to my base and in about two weeks the orders came through. The Battalion Commander called me in and said, "Arthur, what the hell is this?" I told him I hadn't seen the orders, but I guessed I had better follow them, and he reluctantly agreed.

On 3 April 1944, I packed up and travelled up to London where Colonel Gregory assigned me to the office of the Secretary of General Staff. I was a 1st Lieutenant at that time and was assigned to take notes at meetings with General [Omar] Bradley who was in charge of the U. S. land forces and in the process of planning the stages of "Operation Overlord," the invasion of Europe. We knew everything about the plans except the date. They took away our Security Cards and stamped them in big red letters "bigot." I never knew why they chose that word.

Our headquarters was transferred to Normandy about two weeks after D-Day. When the 3rd Army reached the Moselle River east of Verdun, I was summoned to a meeting called by General Patton. General Bradley and General Hasbrouck were there. Patton wanted to relieve the Commanding Officer of the 7th Armored Division and was discussing who should replace him. General Hasbrouck volunteered that he would like the job. Patton said, "You're just the man I had in mind!" and Bradley agreed.

The other officers left and I was alone with General Hasbrouck. I said to the General, "Sir, I heard how you just got that job, and if you need a junior officer with you, I want to be that man." Hasbrouck saw that I was using the same method that he had used and couldn't refuse. So, on 26 September 1944, I became the aide to General Hasbrouck in the 7th Armored Division. (By that time I had been promoted to Captain although I was still only 22.)

The next day we were sent to the Netherlands where we assembled in the vicinity of Eindoven where we joined the British 2nd Army. The Air Borne Troops had landed at Arnhem and Nijmegan, and our assignment was to protect their southern flank and prevent the Germans from coming across the Moselle River. We were given a front of about fifty miles from Overloon to Meijel. We held that front for one month, though the fighting was fierce and we lost a lot of men and equipment. The situation finally stabilized and we were sent to a "rest" area south near Rimburg, Germany, a coal mining town. At the mines our troops had their first shower in a month. New equipment arrived along with replacement troops. But, our promised "rest" never materialized.

Five days later our division received orders to move south. General Hasbrouck had been ordered to report to the 8th Corp at Bastogne in Luxembourg. The MPs had cleared the route, and at one in the morning we started to move. When the General and I finally arrived, the 8th Corp had packed up and left. The Germans were breaking through on a massive fifty-mile front. Bastogne was in the southern corner of their front and the town of St. Vith in Belgium was on the north shoulder. New orders sent us to St. Vith to rescue the 106th Infantry Division which was being decimated. We headed north to the vicinity of Vielsalm to block the Germans from St. Vith, a road center on the north flank of the German attack.

The Division Commander of the 106th was in a terrible foggy state: his son had been captured by the Germans and he had lost two of his three regiments in the battle. General Hasbrouck relieved him and sent him back to the rear.

We fought a fierce battle at St. Vith. Our Combat Command B held the town for seven days, losing men and tanks steadily, out of contact and desperate for reinforcements. General Hasbrouck "volunteered" me to take a message to the 1st Army headquarters. He wrote this out in longhand on a piece of yellow paper and gave me strict instructions to give it to no one but General Bill Kean who was well known by the General and myself. I knew it was a risky mission.

The General's driver Frank Feather and I took off in a jeep which had a machine gun and a wire cutter mounted on the front. We each were armed with hand grenades and had a Thompson submachine gun. After a scary trip, we arrived at the 1st Army headquarters. We were a grungy-looking pair and the MPs weren't going to let us in, but I convinced them of the importance of my seeing General Kean. He was in a meeting with Field Marshall Montgomery, so we waited. I noticed that the door was open, and I could see the General at the table. I stepped to the doorway and turned my left shoulder so that he could see my 7th Armored Division shoulder patch. He noticed and immediately came out and I gave him the message. The General said that they had been very worried about the lack of contact with our division. He told his officer to get us cleaned up and well fed and that he would send a return message.

We left Neuchatel and made the long drive back to a worried General Hasbrouck. General Kean's message said that the 82nd Airborne Division would come up on our left flank and reinforce us.

The next day we made a "daylight withdrawal," always a dangerous move, with some 20,000 men. We had picked up remnants of the 28th Division and the 9th Armored Division. We started before dawn and finished about six that night, getting everyone safely over the one and only small stone bridge over the Salm River.

After our withdrawal from St. Vith, we were sent to Aupen, Belgium, in January 1945, supposedly for some rest. We then got orders to retake St. Vith. It was considered quite an honor to be sent to retake the same town we had been forced to leave. But the German Army had pretty much spent everything they had in the Battle of the Bulge, and there wasn't much resistance. We followed the Germans across the Rhineland where we not only had to contend with the enemy but with the mud, a big problem for an armored unit. In March of 1945, we made it to the Remagen Bridge area. It had been taken by the 9th Armored Division on 7 March and had suffered a lot of damage. Repairs took several days, and we were the fourth and last division to go across right behind my brother's division, the 78th Infantry Division. The bridge then fell into the Rhine River.

From Remagen we went north to the closure of the Ruhr pocket. On the 15th of April, we received a note from a German Army officer who came through the lines with a white flag. The Commander of the 15th Panzer Corp wanted to surrender the Corp and its four divisions. General Hasbrouck decided to send his Chief of Staff, Colonel Ryan, and me to go behind the German lines to negotiate the surrender. We kept in contact with the General by radio and returned that same day with the German commander, General Fritz Bayerlein, a very fine soldier. That was the end of the Ruhr pocket battle.

We were then ordered north over the Elbe River with the British Army to the Baltic Seacoast. We arrived at Lubeck and Travamunde and then proceeded along the Baltic shore and moved east. In a few days we reached a point about sixty miles northwest of Berlin where we were ordered to stop. On May 8, 1945, the war in Europe came to an end with the German surrender.

It seemed a long time before we could get back home. Our division was assigned to occupation duty near Heidelberg. The younger soldiers with fewer points were sent to be re-trained for the Pacific. We were on occupation duty until October when we were sent home on a transport. We were supposed to land in Boston which was great for me because my fiancée, Ann Bailey Draper, could meet me there. Instead, a strike by longshoremen caused us to be diverted to Norfolk. I finally made it back to Boston by train.

That was the end of the war in Europe. It was wonderful to be home, but I was proud to have been there.

A native of Meadville, Pa., Bill graduated from Cornell in 1948 with a BS in engineering. After working for the Norton Company, he became president of Anderson Corp. in Worcester, Mass. He was actively involved in his community, church and the American Red Cross. He and his wife Ann have four children.

Creating the Harbor at LeHavre

Theodore S. Bacon

When I graduated from Amherst College in May 1942, I intended to continue on to M.I.T. where I had been awarded a fellowship in City Planning studies. However, in July 1942, I received a commission as an Ensign in the U.S. Navy Reserves and went to Newport, R.I., for further training.

The Navy thought that my experience as Chief of the Amherst Volunteer Fire Department would qualify me to be assistant fire chief at the U.S. Naval Air Station, Moffatt Field, Calif. I did not want this position, so I continued my training at Newport.

About half way through training, the Navy requested some officers to be part of a new cryptographic unit in New York City at the Port Director's office and I was selected. This work included setting up more secure communications for merchant ships being assigned to convoys bound for England.

In February 1943, the cryptographic unit received a contingent of newly-commissioned WAVE officers fresh from their training at Smith College. I was assigned to help them get started in their coding work. I met one of the WAVE officers, Sarah Hogate, and we were engaged and married in June 1943. Because all military people had to be in uniform, Sarah had to get orders from the Secretary of the Navy to be "out of uniform" to wear her wedding dress!

I stayed in the New York Port Director's office until 1944 when I went to England to work on convoy matters there. After the invasion of France in June 1944, I was assigned to a ship which went over to Omaha Beach to assist in developing port facilities.

As part of the invasion preparations, the Allies constructed three artificial harbors called "Mulberries." Two of these were at Omaha Beach and one at Arromanches, a British beach. The Mulberries provided a dock facility to land men and material from ships anchored offshore. On June 19 and 20, 1944, the largest storm in the English Channel in 30 years destroyed the Mulberries at Omaha Beach, but the one at Arromanches survived.

Although the dock at Arromanches was undamaged, there was still a need for a large and more permanent port capable of handling the massive amount of men and material for the battles to come. The first choice was Antwerp, but it was not captured until late September 1944, and its immediate use was hampered by strong German forces nearby which were not cleared until late November.

Meanwhile, the Allies turned to Le Havre as the major port. The Germans had established a fleet of E-boats at Le Havre, which had been active in harassing ships in the English Channel. After the invasion, the Canadian Air Force bombed Le Harve, killing 5,000 French civilians and demolishing the city and the port. The French government insisted that U.S. forces, and not the Royal Navy, occupy the city and clean it up for use as the major port, and as part of that effort some 16,000 U. S soldiers from the Third Army – including me – cleared most of the wreckage. Among the problems the Allies faced in clearing Le Havre was the presence of a large number of German mines in the water, including sophisticated magnetic mines which proved difficult to remove.

I stayed at Le Havre and Rouen for about 14 months, becoming Assistant Port Director for both cities. During this time I saw many Allied soldiers going into France and, later, many of them going home. Many German prisoners were also moved to the U.S. prison camps.

In December 1945, I returned to the U.S. and joined the staff at Amherst College after two semesters at M.I.T.

Ted was born in Springfield, Mass., and graduated from Deerfield Academy, Amherst College and the Massachusetts Institute of Technology. He was a college professor and dean, and a city and regional planner. He was married to the late Sarah Bacon and they had three children.

The 106th Station Hospital

Jeanne McCutcheon Britton

Wading ashore from a landing craft in Naples, Italy, I could not help but think of the life I had left behind in the mountains of West Virginia. My father was a physician and I had always enjoyed helping with the routines of his office. Becoming a nurse was a lifelong aspiration and I was delighted to enroll in the three year nursing school program at St. Mary's Hospital in Clarksburg, West Virginia. Following Pearl Harbor, Col. Charles S. Fisher (our chief surgeon at the hospital) became the U.S. Army Medical Corps Commanding Officer of the St. Mary's Hospital Unit. I volunteered without hesitation and was commissioned 2nd Lieutenant in the Army Nurse Corps on November 5, 1942.

Before going overseas, I spent nine months of additional training at Lawson General Hospital near Atlanta. From there we were sent to New York City where we joined one of the largest convoys of the war sailing for Oran in Algeria in North Africa. Sharing a small stateroom with 16 other girls called for a bit of tolerance but the food was good and the sea was calm. The requirement to wear life belts and canteens at all times, orders to observe nighttime blackouts, water rationing and limited access to the decks were minor inconveniences.

On arrival in Oran, we were quartered in a somewhat "upscale" part of the city which was tightly guarded. At that time Oran was a crowded, dirty and smelly city. The days were hot and the nights were cold. It was far from a delightful tourist attraction.

I have to say that when we were in Oran, we were really impressed by the work of the Red Cross coping with the challenge of dealing with the needs of both civilian and military populations. However, I can also confess that we were not at all unhappy to leave even though we knew we would be heading into the thick of things in Italy.

Our landing at Naples came just four days after the enemy had retreated from the coast. The bombardment in preparation for the allied landing, coupled with the deliberate demolition of the infrastructure by the German and Italian forces in an effort to slow the invasion, had left a chaotic scene. Our landing was impeded only by the wreckage in the harbor. Once ashore, we were assigned to a building that had been a school. As it turned out, it was a relatively new, unscathed building but the first and second floors were crammed with some dead bodies and a lot of debris. It took us two days to clean out the building and set up our station hospital.

Nurses were billeted in an apartment house nearby where we were quite comfortable with a balcony overlooking the city and surrounding countryside. Nighttime air raids were frequent. Although we were supposed to head for the shelter whenever there was a raid, my curiosity prompted me to watch the action from our balcony. Air raids were not the only attraction. While we were there, Mount Vesuvius erupted and I have some great pictures of that event including a view of the lava flow consuming part of the nearby landscape. It was an awesome sight.

Dealing with patients in rural West Virginia and urban Atlanta was unlike treating the wounded as they came from the battlefields of war. We dealt with everything imaginable - a daunting task. As a station hospital, ours was a second step in a process that could lead to treatment and rehabilitation back in the States. When we established the station hospital we were only four miles or so from the front. Initially we were overwhelmed with refugees and liberated prisoners of war. Battle casualties of course became our most challenging concern. The contribution that we made was reflected in an award of the Meritorious Service Unit plaque that Col. Fisher received for "—for superior performance of exceptionally difficult tasks and outstanding devotion to duty."

Our unit was stationed in Naples for more than two years and during that time I was promoted to the rank of First Lieutenant. Our work at the hospital was arduous but after many months of nursing, I have great memories of a trip to the Isle of Capri for a little R&R. What a change!

Capri was like a "little bit of heaven." You had no sense of a war going on not far away. We had wonderful accommodations and great food. Side trips, sight seeing, swimming and lounging really were therapeutic after ministering to all the victims of conflict.

As the war ended in Europe, we prepared for a new challenge in the Pacific and a landing in Japan. The first leg of that journey was a stop in Hawaii. That, too, was a pleasant but short respite. We soon were at sea again and on our way to set up the 106th Station Hospital on Okinawa. It was here that I experienced one of the miracles of the war. As I was working one day, I was told that a person was looking for me outside of the hospital. That person turned out to be the commanding officer of an Army unit and ... my brother! He had seen the sign for the 106th Station Hospital and knew that was where I was assigned. We had not seen each other in over three years. Being invited to join his unit for dinner that evening and seeing every man in that mess hall stand at attention and salute when I walked in was a memorable experience. We had a great reunion.

It was not long after that we experienced the awesome victory celebration on Okinawa and were headed back to the States. The voyage back was uneventful and the one-month leave I was granted after I returned provided a real welcome home. Although the war was over, my release from active duty was not immediate. After my leave I was assigned to the Ashford General Hospital (also known as the world-famous Greenbrier Hotel) in White Sulphur Springs, W. Va. As you might imagine, duty there was in sharp contrast to our experiences in Naples. We had access to all of amenities of that resort and that is where I was introduced to the game of golf.

Four months later the facility was closed and I was sent to Fort Totten in Bayside, Long Island. At an officers club function there, I met a handsome Coast Guard Captain and not long after, we were married. That was a wonderful finale to my active duty career as an Army nurse. I was released to inactive duty in June of 1947, but as a reservist it was not until June of 1952 that I was officially discharged.

My son has put together a scrapbook of photos and news articles detailing many of the incidents and events of those years. Obviously this has been only a brief summary of my wartime experiences. Although not entirely out of harm's way, I was among the lucky ones to return home with the joys of life ahead marred only by memories of the shattered young men who really sacrificed their lives for our future.

Born in Green Bank, W. Va., Jeanne worked as a registered nurse after serving as an Army nurse during the war. She and her late husband have one child. She spent many years volunteering at the Peterborough Hospital when she lived in the area during the 1980s.

DISPLACED PERSONS IN BONN

ROBERT S. FELLOWS

Pulling out his .45 automatic and slamming it on the desk of the burgomaster, Lt. Butler issued one demand – *wasser*! Butler was carrying out my instructions when our small unit arrived in Bonn with orders to set up a facility to care for displaced persons.

Pointing to his watch and pistol, the lieutenant conveyed the message that the burgomaster would be dead if he didn't get clean water to the German post by 5 p.m. This was a life-or-death matter and it was the beginning of an organized American effort to assist a growing population of liberated prisoners of war and refugees.

I had been the executive officer of a military government detachment which had moved forward to an area west of Cologne after serving near the front during the memorable "Battle of the Bulge." With word that the western part of Bonn had been taken by our First Division, there was a call for a volunteer to lead a small group to start a displaced persons center there. We were informed that this would be a difficult and unusual assignment because of the chaotic conditions involving people in need from Russia, Poland, France, Belgium, Holland and Italy. Disregarding the old army mantra "never volunteer," I immediately opted for the assignment. At that point, I was "stir-happy" with inactivity. My only condition was that I be permitted to pick my own men. Although reluctant to have me leave the unit, my commanding officer approved the assignment and accompanied by Lt. Butler and four enlisted men, equipped with two jeeps, steel helmets and side arms, we headed for Bonn.

We found the First Division headquarters near the center of the city and reported to the G-5 [civil affairs officer] as instructed. The G-5 staff position was established with responsibility for military government in enemy countries and civil affairs in friendly countries. The G-5 said that he could give us no specific instructions and that we would never be asked any questions, for this was to be the first displaced persons center to be operated by Americans in Germany. Our job was to house, feed and take care of these people, and, in so doing, make sure they were "off the streets" and not creating problems or interfering with military operations. Directed to a German army post on the outskirts of Bonn, we found the Polish lieutenant, a liberated prisoner of war himself, now in charge of a small group of others. Fortunately, he spoke good English along with seven other languages which was a great asset in carrying out our mission.

This post overlooked the Rhine River. Artillery was positioned behind us aimed at German targets on the other side of the river. We were pleased to find a First Division infantry unit in place providing security and guarding German weapons and ammunition which had been left behind. The first night we stayed up late developing our plan of organization and operation. The immediate problems were food supply, sanitation and housing. There was little food on hand and American rations were not available for displaced persons. The only water available was in a stagnant fire pool created by the Germans for the purpose of extinguishing incendiary bombs. Due to bomb damage, plumbing was inoperative.

Our instructions to the Polish lieutenant were to designate a leader for each nationality represented by the growing number of displaced persons. In turn, that leader appointed sub-leaders comparable to a military organization. Russian slave laborers comprised about 50% of the displaced persons. The second largest group was Polish. Different nationality groups were assigned to separate buildings. At the outset, men and women were separated, but we found the Russians chose to ignore that edict, which ended our idea of separating the sexes.

The Dutch were given responsibility for preparing and serving the food. Our army cook, Private Biava, was put in charge of this operation. Since the plumbing was not operative, we had trenches dug with screening material to provide some privacy. As described, it was Lt. Butler's strong initiative that helped resolve the water problem. It was known that resourceful Germans would produce under pressure and the threat with the pistol produced a procession of horse-drawn flat wagons loaded with large milk cans of fresh water arriving at just three minutes before five. The use of horses was evidence of the local gasoline shortage.

It was important that we establish high standards of sanitation and cleanliness. After major sanitation problems in the Russian quarters and resistance from the Russian lieutenant in charge, he was "persuaded" to exercise a little military discipline and the situation improved. Visiting generals or other VIP's were always impressed when we showed them the Russian barracks. They assumed that if the Russian quarters were in such good shape, the others must be even better.

That Russian lieutenant became a good friend and we understood each other. The Russian wore a German uniform with a big "P" painted on the back. I wanted to improve his appearance, so found an American quartermaster and prevailed upon him to furnish a U.S. Army uniform. The Russian was pleased and quickly dispensed with the much hated German outfit. He and the Polish leader were invited to join us for meals in our quarters which provided an opportunity to get better acquainted and talk over mutual interests.

Food was a high priority and there was no time for formal requisitions. Remembering the words, "no questions will be asked," we took the most direct method. We sent a couple of GIs to the streets of Bonn to stop and take over civilian trucks which were driven to food warehouses and restaurants. Since looting was rampant in Bonn, we rationalized that displaced persons should have priority on the limited supplies because of their years of Nazi abuse.

In the interest of letting the entire refugee population know that the Americans were in charge and cared for their well being, I prepared a short talk which could be translated for the various languages represented. Climbing onto an empty table in the dining hall, I removed my steel helmet and pistol belt and laid them on the table. When I finished there was loud applause and cheering reflecting an understanding that the Americans really wanted to help and were not like their Nazi oppressors.

An American lieutenant who commanded the infantry unit joined us one evening for "refreshments" and we were somewhat distracted by the unusually large number of shells fired overhead that created a strange whistling sound. Even though we knew the projectiles were not aimed at us, the lieutenant, a victim of battle fatigue, jumped at every shot and said he would rather be on the front lines where he could see what was happening.

The Germans were still holding positions on the east side of the Rhine River and small arms tracers were common sights at night. On one occasion two shells from heavy German artillery exploded nearby. The glass from the window next to me shattered and I looked out to see black smoke billowing into the sky. Fortunately, none of our buildings were hit. Another day a German plane strafed a group waiting to enter the mess hall. A young Russian was hit and bleeding badly. After administering first aid, we rushed him to the Seventh Corp medical unit where he was stabilized and bandaged. Later his big smile expressed his appreciation for the help we had provided.

At the main entrance one day, we saw people wandering away from the post. It was important that they stay until they were adequately prepared for their homeward journey. Responding to surprise secret orders, the First Division had moved out during the night to assist at the Remagan bridgehead. That left us with no guards and no security until U.S. Army trucks were sent. Then we could start shipping people to a safer place where they would be processed for their journey home.

With the displaced persons center established and functioning well ten days after our arrival, we began to realize how much we had accomplished. The Generals and staff officers who were frequent visitors were pleased and complimentary. It was rewarding to see young Russians playing string instruments and dancing on the lawn. One evening about 50 liberated French prisoners of war arrived singing and drinking. By then we had a staff of 50 displaced persons doing well in their positions of responsibility.

On the 22nd of March 1945, a large specialized detachment arrived to replace us so that we could be on our way. This American-trained group included a young Russian officer and others trained for the task. They were honest in noting that their work had already been done by the displaced persons we had organized.

We then headed for Wiesbaden with a feeling that our association with the Europeans had contributed to improving the image of America. On departing the post, some of the leaders gathered around to wish us well. The Dutch, who had handled the food operation so well, shed a few tears. Saying, "*Major sie ist ein grosse mann,*" the Russian lieutenant extended a warm invitation to visit him in Stalingrad after the war and the Polish lieutenant urged me to come and see him in Warsaw. All of this left me with a good feeling.

We prepared the following report for the Seventh Corp Commanding General.

	Persons At The Center	*Transported to Brand, Germany*
Russian	500	1,119
Polish	200	574
French	79	437
Belgian	22	128
Dutch	64	140
Yugoslavs	35	115
Italians	50	42
Greek	0	1
Total	950	2,556

Our unit of six joined the rest of the detachment at Mainz after a five-day assignment in the Remegan bridgehead. On March 28, 1945, we joined our military government unit and waited for a pontoon bridge to be built across the Rhine River at Mainz so that we could cross it and enter Wiesbaden. An infantry company took the city the night before without resistance.

We were the first Americans to be seen by most of the inhabitants. White sheets hung out windows of many apartments along our route to the center of the city.

Although we spent six months establishing a non-Nazi government in Wiesbaden, our days in Bonn left more vivid memories. There we learned that nationality differences could be minimized.

We, as Americans, must greatly improve our understanding of other people of the world if we are to succeed in our peaceful goals.

Born in Manchester, N.H., Bob graduated from the University of New Hampshire where he took the advanced ROTC program and received his commission in the Reserves. After the war, having attained the rank of Lieutenant Colonel, he stayed in the Reserves and continued his career in banking, after attending the Rutgers University Graduate School of Banking. He retired from the Glastonbury Bank & Trust Co. after serving as that institution's president and chief executive officer. He and his wife Carolyn had three children.

THE WAR SEEN FROM BRITAIN

THOMAS H. FORMAN

On September 3, 1939, Britain's then-Prime Minister declared that a state of war existed between Great Britain and Germany. My brother and I had been allowed to enter Great Britain on August 22 of that year as transmigrants, that is, we were allowed to live in England until our quota numbers to enter the United States were reached and we would then move there.

I was the second son of a very close and loving family. I enjoyed a good humanistic education, followed by a few months of collegiate study of textile chemistry. But then my life changed from a possible future as a medical doctor to that of a rather penniless refugee like so many others lucky enough to escape persecution in Hitler's "Thousand Year Reich." Our parents had to wait before they too could escape, which they eventually did.

We were in the drawing room of the British friends of our parents who had enabled our escape. The photograph shows me in the uniform of His Majesties Home Guard, an army of rapid origin to help provide resistance to the attempts of Germany to invade the British Isles. I do not remember when the Home Guard was dissolved. We received intensive training in infantry warfare without leaving our regular occupations. Of course we had to find ways of making a living at the same time. This story is not a personal biography of any sort but an attempt to describe what life in Britain was like during World War II.

Initially I had a number of low-paying basic jobs that ranged from driving delivery trucks and cars for the local stores to working in a machine shop and finding a talent for delicate and accurate work. The firm made various tools for the Navy. My personal adventures during the war were insignificant but witnessing the development and final growth to victory in England was exciting.

My "reserved occupation" job prevented me from joining the fighting forces and of course only after it was all over did I realize how lucky we Home Guard people had been in those first stages of the conflict. The Germans did not invade our islands and, thankfully, we avoided having to fight them with our minimal training and weaponry.

The first few months were called the Phony War when the air raid whistles blew for exercise only to be followed by the all-clear. This soon changed to the Battle of Britain with constant mostly night air raids on cities and industrial installations. The spirit of the people was hard to believe in the way that they took misfortune and rallied to the cause of the war. In all living rooms the picture of King George was displayed along with British flags and the quality of the humor soon far exceeded that of the food. The rationing of food was never a real hardship: It just made one more aware of the common need to support the war effort.

Very dark years followed when the Germans held North Africa with Italy as its partner and huge areas of Europe were in their control. Additionally, rumors of the horrible slaughter of Jews and non-believers were very hard to bear. We did not know the fate of many friends and relatives who had not been able to escape the Nazi fangs. It was a great relief when we got news from our parents from Shanghai whence they had managed to flee.

The wonder of the time for us was Winston Churchill, who proved to be a God-chosen leader who kept our spirits high and was a genius in the way he led the war effort. The Battle of Britain in the air was the first uncertain sign of hope at the price of the lives of many courageous fighter pilots. Living close to the DeHaviland aerodrome, I got glimpses of the "squid," (as I remember the name) the first jet-propelled fighter plane. A time followed of death and destruction with so many victims and such poor prospects of winning over "that guttersnipe," as Churchill called Hitler. Those were long dark months and it was good to work so hard for so many hours and we even felt that our Home Guard were becoming true soldiers under the leadership of our aged officers from World War I.

The fight in the United States to gain wholehearted support for the war effort also left one breathless and when Lend Lease was established and American industry rolled up its sleeves and started to provide increasing numbers of planes and ships, our hopes of final victory were raised. That hope lit up in a bright flame when Hitler declared war on the Soviet Union, which we all saw as a huge blunder that promised the end of the "Thousand Year Reich." Montgomery's victory in North Africa and the collapse of Mussolini's Italy added to the feeling that the dark night of the guttersnipe was perhaps coming to an end.

It is hard to describe the spirit of all one knew in England as it changed from a wonderful sort of cynical acceptance of gloom, doom and death to one of pride and hope. There was still a long, long way to go, but once American troops arrived it was getting clear that Germany had no hope of winning, totally encircled as it was (like in World War I). But the losses and heroic actions of all continued, accompanied by the horrendous loss of life on the part of the enemy, especially the allied air raids that flattened cities like Dresden and Hamburg when literally thousands of people were killed by the firestorms of those attacks. Hiroshima and Nagasaki helped to ensure Allied victory and started many to think sadly of what humans can do to each other from the holocaust to nuclear bombs. It is only to be hoped that in some future of human inner progress this literally earth-destroying game of war will cease.

Born in Brno, Czechoslovakia, Tom graduated from the Masaryk Gymnasium and worked as a mechanical engineer throughout his career. He and his wife Monica have three children. He also did volunteer work for the town of Welwyn Garden City, Hertfordshire, England.

Spy Games After the War

Sym Goodnow

The picture of me was taken early in my career as an Army intelligence specialist at Fort Holabird in Baltimore, Md., where I was part of the base honor guard. I wish I still had my chrome-plated helmet to wear around RiverMead.

The year was 1959. In December Molly and I were married in Erie, Pa. I was then studying the Russian language at the Presidio in Monterey, Calif. This was a year-long course for six hours a day. After about seven months, I was surprised to discover that I was fairly fluent in the language. At the end of that year, we were moved to Stuttgart, West Germany, where we lived for two years. I served with the Army Counter Intelligence Corps. Molly, who had worked for the CIA in Washington prior to our marriage, was useful with her CIA security clearance and worked for my boss.

1960-61 were years of great tumult in East Germany, with hundreds of thousands of refugees fleeing to West Berlin and West Germany to free themselves from the Communist oppression and dire poverty. A similar exodus also began from other Communist-dominated eastern European countries. This crush of refugees had to be controlled and provided for by the U.S. and Allied forces in Western Europe. It was necessary to screen and document as many of these refugees as possible and to try to resettle them. At that time, Canada and Australia were both willing to accept refugees and others were processed through to the United States.

It became apparent early on that the refugee populations were being infiltrated by agents of the Communist Eastern Bloc countries posing as normal refugees with the purpose of gaining re-settlement in Western countries where they could then act as secret operatives for their Communist handlers. It was also discovered that there were frequent border crossers who came to West Germany to gain information concerning U.S. Army troop movements and strengths. Having made their observations, they would return surreptitiously to the East to report their findings and then recross to the West with new instructions. A number of these individuals were infamous for the frequency of their crossings. Some of them were apprehended and incarcerated. Others were successfully "flipped," or persuaded to work for the West, and sent back East to gather intelligence for us. Most of these operatives were motivated by money, not ideology, and several were caught working both sides as triple agents, a very dangerous pursuit.

At my unit's headquarters in Stuttgart, we had all of the intelligence records for the U.S. Army in southern West Germany, plus many of Hitler's intelligence files. Of course, we had no computers but only a system of file folders (by the thousands) and index cards. Our unit would receive requests for information on particular individuals from our own field offices, other allied military units, U.S. embassies and the consulates of western allies. For most inquiries about refugees, the search would produce nothing of interest.

My job was to ferret out the bad guys. As a Russian linguist, I was able to assist interpreting the Cyrillic alphabet soup we were dealing with and we had varied degrees of success. "Dimitri Ivanovsovich," when translated to English from Cyrillic, might produce a half dozen spellings, which resulted in a half dozen different files and file reference cards, each of which by themselves looked totally normal and harmless. Upon bringing all those files together, a very different picture and potentially dangerous character might emerge. My biggest success involved a refugee who had been cleared for immigration to Australia. My subsequent investigation of his several files showed him to be a frequent border crosser and probable Communist agent. I received a letter of commendation from the Australian government for my efforts.

Born and raised in Keene, N.H., Sym graduated from Dartmouth College and the Boston University School of Law. He spent 45 years as a practicing attorney and did extensive volunteer work in Keene. He and his wife Molly have two children.

Gathering Storm

Louise Guion

It was 1932. Roosevelt had just been elected President. My sister and I were still in bed recovering from the measles. Mother came into our room and laid out a diagram of a large ship and told us that Dad had a sabbatical year and we were going to Europe. I was so excited! She then showed us where our staterooms would be. We would sail in February.

The day we were to leave my sister was sick with a fever. After much talk it was decided that we would go. My parents had acquired a second-hand car, a rather large LaSalle. This, as we found out later, was rather difficult to drive on the narrow Italian roads. However, it was useful for the traveling we expected to do. So we packed up and headed for New York. The name of our ship was the *Counte de Savoia*. It was a new ship and the pride of the Italian fleet.

We had a rough trip over and were glad to see Gibraltar. I understand the ship was used as a troop ship later and was probably sunk. We landed in Genoa the day that Roosevelt closed the banks. My sister was still sick so we stayed in Genoa for almost a month. I got to see a lot of the city and rode the funicular up the mountain every day. Finally the U. S. bank was able to send us money. The hotel never asked questions. We thought maybe they were impressed by our large American car.

We traveled down the west side of Italy, seeing all the usual sights including Pompeii. While in Rome we saw and heard Mussolini at the Victor Emmanuel Monument. It was very crowded and noisy. In Bologna we saw the young boys in their uniforms marching with their wooden rifles. Eventually we reached Munich. We were very aware of Hitler as his headquarters were in Munich. We boarded with the Ortels—friends of my grandparents as he taught Sanskrit at Yale.

Every day on our walk we passed the military building pontoon bridges across the Isar River. And every night they took them down and started all over again in the morning.

My father and Uncle Hans would sit side by side in the middle of the garden talking. In retrospect, I think they were afraid their conversations would be overheard. My father had been in charge of a field hospital in France in the first war and he was very concerned about the future.

I have many memories about this trip and still love to travel. As it turned out we came home in September as my grandfather was ill and he died shortly after our return.

Born in New Haven, Conn., Louise graduated from Vassar College in 1945 and spent her career in the social services. Among her favorite causes were the League of Women Voters, Litchfield Community Services and the Girl Scouts. She and her husband had five children.

The Convoys of Sierra Leone

René Isaac

When World War II broke out in 1939, I was a 15-year-old schoolboy in England attending a Quaker coeducational boarding school. We had our own fire brigade and trained with firemen from a nearby town who came on weekends because we had an enormous macadam playground for drills. We were also organized to help the farmers at harvest time and go off to summer camp to pick fruit. Otherwise the impact of the war on my life was minimal.

The German invasion of France and Belgium and the evacuation of the British Army from Dunkirk changed everything. The possibility of a German invasion brought the war to the home front. My parent's house on the Cornish coast of the English Channel overlooked a sandy beach perfect for landing craft. It was in a valley about a mile from the village and consisted of about 20 houses of which only four were occupied in the winter. The army came and built cement teeth to make a landing more difficult. My 56-year-old father joined the Home Guard and went off at night with his rifle to keep watch. Obviously a great deterrent to a possible invasion!

I came home from school for the holidays. There were times when I'd climb the hill behind our house and see the glow in the sky from the night bombing of the dockyards in Plymouth fifteen miles away. One day after a winter storm I was walking the beach and saw large bales of raw rubber that had washed up from a sunken merchant ship. With help we retrieved many bales and stored them in our garage. The Coast Guards were notified and came and took them away. Later we received a generous payment for our efforts.

With the heavy bombing of London the authorities arranged for many children to be evacuated to the countryside. My parents always wanted a daughter and happily became foster parents of a young girl. Because she was brought up as an Irish Catholic the local priest would come to check that our Quaker family was properly looking after her. Mysteriously, he always turned up at tea time. After the war her parents, who had separated, never came to take her back and she became a permanent member of the family. Strong minded and very determined, she succeeded in business, married and had three great children. We keep in touch and visited her the last time we were in England.

In the summer of 1943 I was called up and joined the Royal Navy, a step that was expected of me as a young man growing up in a fishing village. I was sent to H.M.S. *Ganges* near Ipswich, East Anglia for basic training. After twelve weeks I graduated as an ordinary seaman and was sent to the Portsmouth naval base to await assignment. I had the unique experience of serving on H.M.S. *Victory*, Nelson's flag ship. I scrubbed the decks and saw various dignitaries come to visit including Queen Wilhelmina of the Netherlands. Finally I was sent to Liverpool with my duffle bag and hammock to join the sloop H.M.S. *Folkstone*.

Following a shake-down cruise, the ship joined a convoy bound for South Africa and Asia. When we reached Freetown, Sierra Leone, we were detached from the convoy and it became our base of operations. We went on convoy duty running along the west coast of Africa to Lagos, Nigeria. We saw no sign of the enemy, no guns fired in anger, just tropical heat, boredom and anti-malaria pills, which gave one a yellow hue.

As the new recruit, I was given the most menial jobs, one of which was scrubbing the deck over the engine room in shorts and a mat to protect my knees from the heat. I had been selected after basic training as a potential officer candidate and in theory I was to be sent to the naval academy after six months. On the ship I received special instructions and because of this, the crew were well aware of my special situation and not unhappy about giving me some of the more onerous tasks. However, after about six months I became accepted as an OK kid and one of them.

In the Royal Navy, every sailor over the age of 21 got a rum ration—officially one part rum to two parts water. On the small ships this was overlooked and they got their rum straight. Some would store it up for special occasions and use it as a form of currency. Favors were paid for by "sippers" or "gulpers." I was not old enough to draw a rum ration but I knew I was accepted when some fellows offered me some of theirs. The Navy finally canceled the rum ration in 1970. Incidentally the officers had their duty-free liquor when in harbour. American naval officers did not have this benefit but did on occasion come on board British ships for cocktails.

After fifteen months, by now an Able Seaman, I was sent back to England on a troop ship to go to the King Alfred Naval Academy. I graduated from the academy as a Sub Lieutenant R.N.V.R. I was sent to Northern Ireland to get instruction in ASDICS—antisubmarine sonar equipment. While playing rugby for the ship H.M.S. *Loch Fada* I injured my knee and got a certificate to show for my efforts. My training over, I was sent home to await orders from the Admiralty. I was directed to join a troop ship in Liverpool for posting to Freetown, Sierra Leone. Obviously some brilliant mind in the Admiralty Offices in London had decided that Isaac was an expert on West Africa and must be sent back.

In Freetown I joined the H.M.S. *Inkpen*, a converted coal-burning, ocean-going fishing trawler with four officers and a crew of about 70. Our job was to participate in coastal convoys. Our departure was delayed, however, because we awaited a new Captain—the incumbent was ashore in hospital with D.T.s.

My duties included serving as antisubmarine officer, navigator, code book security, wardroom supplies and, most importantly, rotating officer of the watch. We had no fancy electronics equipment to determine our position so as navigator I relied on my sextant to take star sightings to calculate our positions. Fortunately, in the tropics one generally has clear skies and plenty of stars to choose from.

I remember well with our new Captain now onboard and leaving harbour for the first time he turned to me and said, "Isaac, once we clear the boom you will be watch officer in charge of the ship. If you have any concerns call me." In wartime you have to take responsibility at an early age—perhaps one is almost too young to realize how much. Fortunately I was smart enough to recognize as a wartime officer that the oil that keeps the machinery of war running smoothly are the career NCOs; in my case the Petty Officers.

Our convoy duties came to an end with the end of the war in Europe. We were ordered back to England and decommissioned in Hull, Yorkshire. I was sent home and received orders relieving me of my commission. It was time to go to college and take advantage of the British equivalent of the G.I. Bill. I count myself as one of the lucky ones.

Born in Liskeard, Cornwall in England, René graduated from the London School of Economics in 1949. He spent his career at the Reader's Digest Company, rising from Research Manager to vice president of corporate planning and new business. He and his wife Ann have three children and five grandchildren.

A Witness at Buchenwald

Robert D. Johnson

About four miles from Weimer, Germany, on a little heavily wooded hill is one of the largest German prison camps, Buchenwald. One Sunday morning, 15 April 1945, when I was stationed at Weimer, I visited this camp and spent about three hours there seeing the unbelievable suffering and torture that these people had been through. There were only 20,000 prisoners there then, but at capacity the camp held about 60,000.

The area looked somewhat like an Army camp, at least from a distance. It was surrounded by a double-wire fence with guard houses at intervals. As we walked through the gate I noticed a large black flag on the flagpole at the entrance. Later, one of the prisoners told us it was in honor of our dead President Roosevelt [who had died three days earlier]. Above the gate was a sign that said: "Right or Wrong, it is for Germany."

The buildings were about the size of an Army barracks, some two-story concrete structures, and others one-story wood-framed buildings. Most of the latter were originally horse stables. In a space where we would put about 60 men they had crammed 1,000. That day, there were about 200 men in these rooms. Along the sides there were shelves about six feet deep on which they lived and slept. They were three deep on each side with about a five-foot aisle through the center. The prisoners of this camp were men and boys from the conquered countries, mostly Polish and French.

All of them were supposedly political enemies of the Nazi party, charged with sabotage or underground activities or refusal to work. Some of them were undoubtedly innocent, but most of them would tell you how they worked against Nazism before they were caught. The oldest men were probably about 60 years old and among the few boys there was one two-years old and several that were six or eight. The older men would point to these boys and say, "He is a dangerous criminal," or "He would not work for Hitler." These men shared their rations with the boys and took care of them so they were in comparatively better physical condition. These people were incarcerated there for various periods of time, some as long as 10 or 12 years and some only a few months. The camp itself was 12 years old.

As we went through the gate one of the prisoners who seemed well educated and spoke fluent English came up to guide us around. He had been there about 18 months and was from Holland.

The first building he took us through was the latrine, a long building with just an open trough about 10 feet deep down through the center. There were poles along both sides for them to sit on. As we walked through, the stench was terrific and the floor was littered by the ones who were too weak to get to the trough.

Next we went to a building where the weakest ones, slowly dying from dysentery and normal starvation, were kept. About 60 percent of the dysentery cases died because they had no medicine or even suitable food to counteract it. In the few minutes we were there they carried out two men who had died. There were several men who just walked through lifting up the blankets to see if the patients were still alive. All in this building were just living skeletons. They lifted one out of the bunk so we could see. He was too weak to stand and we could see every bone in his body through the skin that was stretched over it. When we walked out the guide showed us a little shed beside the building in which there were six or eight bodies piled up waiting to be carried to the crematory. They didn't have any clothes on as all the clothing was removed and saved for someone else.

We walked on through some more of the living quarters and over to the regular hospital. It had some equipment but was not at all adequate and there was not any medicine or drugs. There were barracks for patients with tuberculosis, typhus and other communicable diseases. The guide told us that very few of the prisoners ever were taken to this hospital; it was mostly for the SS troops who were guards there.

From the hospital we went out to the crematory where the bodies were burned. This was about the cleanest part of the camp. There were six sections in the furnace; each section would burn two bodies at a time, in about 20 minutes. There were still some charred bones in the furnace. They had not been used for the past few months because of lack of fuel. Instead the Germans just dug deep pits and had mass burials. Above the furnace was a nice plaque on which was written in German: *I loved the warmth and the light, so burn me, don't bury me.*

In the basement of the building we were shown where the victims were brought in and hanged. Most of the people were taken there alive and hanged before they were burned. When they were too weak or too sick to work, they were brought here to be disposed of. Although they had been taken down before we arrived, we were told that in this basement were 48 hooks around the wall, with a rope for each one. The rope was placed around the victim's neck and then he was lifted up and the other end was fastened to these hooks. Since there was no drop or sudden jar to break their necks they just hung there until they were choked to death. When they had a lot to execute in this manner they sometimes took them down before they were dead and threw them on a pile in the corner to be carried up on the lift. If any of them got up from the pile they had a club there to beat them back down. As many as 600 prisoners would be disposed of here in a single day.

The death rate in the camp was very high, both from natural death and the hangings in the crematory. During the month of March this year [1945], 6,000 died there. At the time Poland fell and the Polish prisoners were coming in, the death rate reached its peak of 900 in a single day. This was during cold weather and the prisoners had little or no clothing, so they were dying from exposure.

When these prisoners were brought in or moved from one camp to another they were stripped of their clothing and forced to march through the streets of the cities and on the trains naked.

We asked the guide why some of them, even though they had been there a long time, were still in better condition than others. He said it was according to the sickness they had and one of the main factors was their morale. Once they lost their morale they just wasted away. He himself had had dysentery for four days and somehow or other recovered from it and he also showed us ugly scars on his legs where he had been injured and infection had set in. He had suffered from high fever and been very sick, practically dead for several months. When he came into the camp he weighed about 180 pounds and now weighed about 120. During his sickness he had been down to less than 100.

It is not hard to understand how so many starved to death. It is harder to believe they could live on what they had to eat. Their daily ration consisted of a small piece of black bread the thickness of your thumb and a pat of margarine the size of three sticks of gum. Then they were given a bowl of soup which was nothing but slop, unseasoned and barely cooked. This guide said the first couple weeks they couldn't stand to eat it but later became accustomed to it. In the barracks where they slept on the shelf-like bunks, they would hide a dead man for several days so they could get the food placed in his hand each day. We went through the kitchen in which this food was prepared; there were several rows of large vats for making the soup.

Outside the camp there were factory buildings in which the prisoners were forced to work. Most of the factories had been knocked out by our bombers. It was a good example of our precision bombing. In flattening these factories, only two bombs had dropped inside the camp where they lived, less than 100 yards away. Of course many prisoners were killed while working in the factories at the time of the bombing but, the guide said, to them death was a welcome release.

The guide told us many stories about the terrible crimes that were committed there. For instance the SS men would occasionally pick out a prisoner with fair, clear skin at the weekly inspections. The man would be killed and his skin taken for lamp shades for the Camp Commandant's wife.

The SS guards were a ruthless bunch of killers and these people really hated them. As we were leaving the camp that day we got out into the woods a little ways and some of the prisoners that had been released were coming out of the woods with an SS man they had found hiding there. He was certainly well beaten up. They don't want to see the SS killed, believing death would be too easy an escape.

The SS would have drunken parties quite frequently and would sometimes take three or four prisoners over to the hospital and dissect them just for the "fun" of carving them up.

Last night we listened to the War Report broadcast over the CBS in which they told about this camp. Maybe you have heard it. The commentator said, as one of the prisoners had told him "To be able to write about it you must have been there for two years, after that you couldn't write about it." These are the living dead.

Author's Note: This article, which I wrote in May 1945 after visiting Buchenwald German prison camp, has been given to Keene State. It was displayed and is stored in the Mason Library, Cohen Center for Holocaust Studies. I kept a copy for myself and gave a copy to all of our family. I was there as a medic the day after the camp had been liberated and the prison guards had fled.

Born in Galesburg, Ill., Robert grew up on his father's cattle farm in Rhame, N. Dak. He is a graduate of the University of Illinois and spent his career as a Certified Property and Casualty Underwriter. He volunteered with the Boy Scouts, the prison ministry, served as a volunteer fireman and EMT and helped build and maintain hiking trails. He and his wife Dean had two children.

The Invasion of Normandy

John M. Keefe

Our ship was the USS *Somers*, DD 381, a destroyer or destroyer leader built in 1937, some said with funds FDR purloined from other parts of the then-small military budget. She was 381 feet in length and 38 feet in the beam, driven by steam turbines of enormous horsepower. She had a top speed of about 45 knots.

We had about 300 enlisted men and petty officers and 20 commissioned officers, plus usually five or more visiting officer specialists. This crew was at least a third more than the ship had been designed for, and new crewmen were expected to sleep on the deck in any space they could find until they became senior enough to rate a bunk or a hammock.

The *Somers'* armament in 1944 was eight 5-inch .38 caliber guns in four unarmored turrets, two forward and two aft. These were controlled from a director over the bridge and pilot house. This was a mechanical version of what we would now call a computer, tied into our fire control radar and extremely accurate, taking into account ship and target speed, the roll of the ship, weather, etc.

Our anti-aircraft defense consisted of eight 20 millimeter Oer- likon machine guns mounted throughout the ship. Controlling the crews on these was my battle station responsibility as Assistant Gunnery Officer. The range of these guns was about 2,000 yards, but if a plane got that close, it was too late to stop it.

Since eight of the five-inch guns could theoretically fire about 30 shells per minute, the ship could launch a devastating barrage at any surface or shore target within nine or ten miles. No destroyer had any armor and our 3/8th inch plating would do nothing to stop a well aimed shell or bullet. It was because of our obsolete armament that we assumed, as we anticipated being in the invasion of Europe, that the *Somers* would be sent in to engage the German shore batteries at close range. This was a prospect that filled us with considerable trepidation when we knew the invasion was on, even though we were accustomed to the dangers of U-boat attack.

Our Normandy story really began when we left New York, May 14, 1944 with a relatively fast convoy. Included in the escort group were five new 2200-ton six-gun Fletcher-class destroyers. We did not know anything about any invasion of France or northern Europe, although we assumed that there would be one at some point. The convoy was just another convoy.

We made landfall in Scotland and moored in the immense roadstead at Greenock which was filled with ships. We had a liberty and went into Glasgow. I remember the cold, bleak weather and city, the good strong black tea at a canteen, and the kindness of a Scottish lady who offered us some of her precious clothing coupons when she saw us looking at tartans in a store window. We declined but were much touched, knowing that our destroyer quarters were much warmer than anything she had during the war.

Back on the ship, we officers were briefed on the invasion in the wardroom. We felt the drama. It was the big show. There were piles of documents detailing ship movements of 4,000 craft from the many invasion ports to the staging areas in the English Channel opposite the invasion area, charts showing the lanes of traffic for the craft moving towards the beaches, and charts and maps of the invasion beaches and coastal Normandy. We officers spent hours locked in the wardroom making corrections on these documents. The crew was told, since there was to be no further shore liberty for anyone.

We were then sent down the Irish Sea, escorting the *Nitro*, an ammunition ship, to the harbor of Milford Haven in Wales. It was there that a Catholic priest came on board and said Mass. It was a mob scene and I have surmised that many of us, not ordinarily observant, had suddenly felt the need to cover our bets.

The invasion plans showed the *Somers* arriving at the beachhead at D+1, but did not specify her duties thereafter. We were not listed as part of the two groups of fire support ships that would initially go to the Omaha and Utah beaches, but were part of the reserve fire support group, consisting of the British cruiser Augusta and 17 U.S. destroyers.

We were nevertheless apprehensive since we expected that the German ship batteries would be more effective than they were. Traditionally, ships without armor fare badly against pillboxes and properly casemated shore artillery. We expected that we would be thrown against the formidable German shore batteries or used for close-to- shore covering fire for the troops when the other ships had been hit or exhausted their ammunition.

The *Somers* was capable of providing an accurate, devastating barrage of 5-inch shells equivalent to a much larger number of army guns. But this main battery was obsolete, useless against aircraft, and the ship had to be rebuilt, almost from the hull up. Therefore, not being more than ordinarily brave, we were justifiably worried that we would be thrown in where it was most dangerous.

We were not worried about the Luftwaffe, as the squadrons of British Spitfires kept control of the air and we knew that no major German warships could or would attack. Submarines and German E- boats were a concern.

The invasion timetable was delayed a day by a storm and on June 5 we were sent around Lands End and went into the crowded harbor of Plymouth where we drifted back onto a mooring buoy chain, damaging a propeller. We listened to the resulting vibration, some of us with hopes of being sent to a yard for repairs.

We spent the eve of D-Day, June 6, in Plymouth and heard flights of aircraft overhead, hundreds of them, some towing gliders, some with our parachute troops. We knew that they would have heavy casualties.

On D-Day, June 6, 1944, we put out of Plymouth with a slow convoy. It was a gray day following the gale that had delayed the invasion by 24 hours and we headed for a large assembly area off the Isle of Wight where the invasion fleet turned to the French coast. As we proceeded, we got a sonar contact with a U-boat, we thought, and dropped depth charges. Debris surfaced with what looked to be human torsos in life jackets. I was almost sick. We stopped and pulled one in with a grappling line, intending to confirm our kill. It was a bale of meat: We had depth-charged a sunken freighter.

As we neared our assembly area, the sea and horizon were lined with troopships, warships, freighters, landing craft, obsolete ships to be sunk to make artificial harbors and "Mulberries," immense floating caissons that looked like floating apartment buildings. These too, we knew from the plans, were to be part of the artificial harbor works at the beaches. We spent the night at battle stations, slowly moving with our convoy to arrive at the invasion beaches on D-Day+1 as scheduled.

As we approached the enormous beachhead that gray morning, D-Day+1 of the invasion, June 7, 1944, we could see most of the French invasion coast and hundreds of the ships in the invasion armada. We heard that two destroyers had been lost, but little else on the actual progress of the invasion. Spitfires were flying formations high above the invasion fleet, giving us a warm feeling.

With our binoculars, we could see buildings of small French ports, wrecked landing craft, the artificial harbors that had been established in the area of Omaha beach and the British beaches, and supplies and men being unloaded. There seemed to be little activity on the Utah beachhead on the Cherbourg peninsula. Some of our ships could be seen shelling inland targets. Artillery fire could be heard but we could not see any fighting, our troops having forced their way inland.

As an Assistant Gunnery Officer, I had been tasked with being the ship's expert on plane identification. I had worked quite hard on it, appreciating that it was important to spot an enemy plane, it being considered bad form to shoot at just anything in the air. In fact, the invasion plans were most adamant as to not shooting at our own planes. To make this simpler for all, our planes were all to be specially marked with broad black and white stripes on each wing, in addition to their usual markings.

The Captain was standing beside me when we spotted a plane coming at us low and quite close to the water. At this point the plane looked like at least one of the German models and we trained the guns we had manned on it. The Captain and I were both of a mind not to give the plane the benefit of the doubt. Luckily, the pilot apparently saw or sensed our apprehensions and nosed up so that we could see the stripes on his wings. He probably was not in great danger since hitting him with our 5-inch shells or even the 20s would have required almost blind luck.

We loitered about the invasion area during the day of June 7, reasonably concerned about mines, studying the coastal towns and beaches, listening to the artillery fire inland and some firing by ships. Planes during the day were not a concern, since we had heavy air cover, mostly flights of British Spitfires. Mines were a worry, even though the area had been swept, but about all we could do was keep a sharp lookout for any that might be floating on the surface.

The First Night

That night, June 7/8, and for much of the remainder of our tour at Normandy, we were assigned to the "Mason-Dixie line," a picket line of our lighter ships. The Mason part of this line ran out about 2-3 miles from the Cotentin (Cherbourg) Peninsula, and then angled easterly to become the Dixie line. The two lines shielded the ships at the Utah and Omaha beaches, until it joined a similar British line. With us on the line, which ran about seven miles from the shore, were twelve other U.S. destroyer escorts and some other PT boats and PCs, backed up by four more U.S. destroyers, three British and a British DE.

We were the screen for the U.S. invasion force and intended to guard the force against German E-boats, fast 50-60-foot torpedo craft like our PTs, armed with torpedoes and 40 mm cannons, believed to be based at Cherbourg along the coast. German destroyers and subs were another threat.

The action that night began for us at darkness, about midnight, with enormous fireworks along all the invasion beaches, a curtain of fire with tracers of all colors, flares and bursting anti-aircraft shells. We assumed it was mostly response to Luftwaffe attacks, the Luftwaffe lying doggo in the day when the sky was owned by our planes.

I recall particularly hearing a string of blasts on shore that echoed in our hull and being grateful that I was not on the beach under them. We were not at general quarters (battle stations) at the beginning of the night, but about 0100 general quarters was sounded. We were trained to get to our battle stations on the run, in a fraction of a minute for most of us. My battle station was control of our eight 20 mm machine guns by telephone from the overhead (roof) of the bridge and pilot house, up four ladders (steep stairs) from the main deck. I could see or hear most of what went on in the pilot house and on either wing of the bridge. On the same platform was the controller for a main 5-inch battery, a revolving nine-foot square housing that held the five persons running the main battery controller, a massive mechanical computer that controlled the main battery. I had about the best seat in the house.

As I raced up the ladders to my station, some of the other DDs [destroyers] were firing out from the Dixie line. From eavesdropping on the voice radio transmissions, I learned that they believed they were shooting at E-boats showing on their radars. We picked up the targets on our radar and joined in with a number of salvos. When we fired our salvos, the entire ship shuddered violently from the shock of the gunfire and recoil, and the flashes from the eight guns lit up the night and the smoke from the muzzles. The smell of gunpowder lingered in the night breeze. Star shells lit up the sea, but not enough to allow us to see E-boats that were more than a mile (2,000 yards) away.

It was heady, exciting action even for spectators like myself. We did not believe we had hit anything, but we apparently had discouraged the E-boat attack and were gung-ho for more action.

Early in the morning hours of June 8, the Luftwaffe came low over the screen, much closer, we knew, than any friendly planes would come at night. A number of ships in the screen opened fire and one plane came over us plainly visible in the glare from tracers. I gave the order to fire our 20 mms over the telephone that connected me with each gun. The tracers were glorious, but the target passed over without being hit, not surprisingly. Farther off, a ship, somewhat behind our picket line and off Utah beach, became an inferno.

In the morning of June 8, the DD *Glennon* hit a mine off Utah beach, with 29 killed. She then came under fire from German shore batteries, and was sunk by them the next day while salvage attempts were being made. The DE *Rich* came up to her to see if she could help and then hit a mine herself, breaking in two with three large explosions and sinking, with 89 killed. We were not generally given any count at that time of the killed and wounded.

The Second Night

On our second night at the invasion, June 8/9, battle stations were sounded at about midnight, when it became dark, and there was another E-boat attack, but not on our part of the screen. During these nights, we spent the dark hours at our battle stations. I was pleased to find that with adrenalin, and perhaps youth, and a few hours of sleep during the day when not on watch, I had no problem staying alert.

The next warm action occurred on the night of June 11/12, when overcast conditions created a black night, with about 2,000 yards visibility. We were about 1,600 yards from the DD *Nelson* and the DD *Laffey* was on her other side on the picket line. About 0105, we picked up radar contacts at about 8,000 yards and opened fire with starshells and common at about the same time as the *Nelson* and the *Laffey*. The three ships fired a number of salvos without any clear hits. We then heard over the voice radio that the *Nelson* had been torpedoed. We thought from these reports that she had lost only three or four people and was operational but she had 24 killed when the torpedo blew off her stem and after gun mount.

It was later that night when we and most of the rest of the screen picked up another radar target coming in fairly slowly. There was much American chatter on our voice radios between the four or five DDs that were tracking the craft, when suddenly a very British voice said, "I say, are you fellows talking about us?" I wonder if he knew how close he was to getting a barrage of 5-inch shells.

We then were sent back to the screen. On the night of June 13/14, there was heavy anti-aircraft fire again and several planes were hit making blossoms of fire in the sky. One plane came over closely and dropped a bomb. It was not a near miss but close enough so that we felt the concussion and the blast.

Days were quiet. One pleasant day we were close to Utah beach and I watched our soldiers working along the shore with flame throwers. We were not even at battle stations. When my watch was relieved, I went down into the wardroom and ate off our usual tablecloths and silver. It was better by far than being in the infantry. I understood how Pearl Harbor happened, since a German plane from the Cherbourg peninsula could have been over us when we only had a couple of 20s manned. Of course, even all eight would not have been much help.

This was the end of Normandy for us but I do recall seeing some of the force that attacked Cherbourg on June 25 come limping back after taking heavy German shelling. Three of our DDs, the *Texas* and the HMS *Glasgow* were hit with the loss of 14 men.

Our next action was to be the invasion of southern France and we headed for the Mediterranean.

Born in Clinton, Iowa, John graduated from the Bronxville, N. Y. high school, Dartmouth College and the Yale Law School. He worked as an attorney his entire career. He served as board member and treasurer of Monadnock Music, was a school board member for the Wilton-Lyndeboro School Board and served on the board of the N.H. Transportation Authority. He and his wife Ann had four children.

The 10th Mountain Division in Italy

F.O. Lathrop

It was December 7, 1941, when I was a freshman at Williams College, that the the bombing of Pearl Harbor took place. I knew that I would be headed for the Army or Navy. I soon learned that my eyes were not good enough to be a pilot in the Air Corps, but also found that with three letters of recommendation I could join a new branch in the Army determined to become mountain troops.

After watching Finland hold up the Russians so effectively, General George C. Marshall decided to create a new mountain division.

It started at Fort Lewis [Washington state] near Mount Rainer with newly recruited skiers, mountain climbers from here and Europe, and outdoorsmen. They made up the 87th Regiment. The 86th and 85th Regiments were later recruited and trained at a new Camp Hale in Colorado situated at 9,500 feet, surrounded by 11,000-foot peaks.

While the 85th and 86th Regiments were training at Camp Hale, the 87th was sent to the Aleutians to take Kiska Island from the Japanese. They made amphibious landings in heavy fog only to find, when the fog lifted, that the Japanese had left the island. Our forces remained there for four months before returning to join the other regiments at Camp Hale.

In March of 1944 in heavy snow and -30°F nights, the division ran a very severe and testing "D" Series to prove their mountain capabilities under extreme conditions.

But our training was not over. In June of 1944 the regiments moved down to Camp Swift, Texas for jungle training with the poisonous snakes and bugs that were there. I actually woke up one morning with a black widow spider in bed with me. I was not bitten but I immediately secured a hammock and stayed off the ground.

General George P. Hays took over the 10th Mountain Division in November 1944 and we headed for Italy on January 7, 1945, docking in a bombed-out Naples. From there the regiment moved up the coast to Leghorn (close to Pisa) and took up positions near the Gothic Line where the Germans had twice successfully repulsed Allied attacks. Patrols were sent to feel out enemy positions.

We faced a line of peaks over 3,000 feet high that ran generally east-northeast and as they approached the Po Valley dropped in height, ending in a broad plain on either side of the Po River. As we reached the Lake Garda area, the mountains became large and precipitous.

Our initial attack plan was to climb the steep Riva Ridge at night using fixed ropes and surprise the enemy at first light. Thanks to some good fortune there was heavy fog when our troops overran some very surprised Germans. We took and held the ridge from ensuing counter attacks.

This position gave us observation over the German positions on Mount Belvedere. From here on it was attack, take another set of peaks, reorganize with wounded, get replacements, send POWs back, rest a bit and repeat the process to the Po River. We continued north to Lake Garda where we were held up with blown tunnels along the lake and heavy fighting before finally taking Tarboli and Nago. On May 2nd, at 1840 hours, General Von Vietinghof's forces of northern Italy surrendered. We remained in Italy, watched Tito carefully and took troops to the Austrian-Yugoslavian border. I missed a chance to climb Mont Blanc when my company was called back to return to the U.S.A.

While we were crossing the Atlantic for a stopover in the U.S. before continuing on to Japan, the first A-bomb was dropped on Hiroshima. We had docked at Hampton Roads and I was en route home when the second bomb was dropped and the war was over.

Born and raised in Fall River, Mass., Francis spent most of his business life with Nashua Corp. With his wife, the former Cynthia Taft, he lived in Amherst, N.H. and raised their four children and now has 17 grandchildren. In January 2011, Francis married the former Betty Billipp at RiverMead.

THE DESERTED VILLAGE

BRUCE McCLELLAN

Just before reaching La Spezia on the coastal road south of Genoa one passes through a mountainous area. Tiny villages are hidden in ribbon-like valleys that thread between high, wooded ridges. In one of these we a passed a deserted village. I could imagine that it had once been the happy home for some two or three hundred families. This had been their world. With all the unhappiness to which mortals are subject, with all the hardness of this poverty-stricken life, this was a place where they could sink their roots deep into the soil.

Now the village is deserted. It is not as though they had chosen to leave for better places. This is not a village like those ghost towns of our American west where one mining strike after another led to mercurial growth and decline of frontier settlements. No, bombs, shells, and bullets have forcefully wrenched them from their native soil. The small stone bridge was probably the first to go. Two or three five-hundred pounders reduced it to rubble, and the women of the village could no longer do their laundry on the steps before the bridge. Wooden door frames and windows burned away. Roofs splintered down on to hearths, giving them fuel of a new sort. Human blood was sacrificed to the war god, but that mattered little because life had already fled.

Four years ago to this day I had a tail gunner, name of Bob. Age: nineteen. Height: five feet and eight inches. Disposition: happy. He could impersonate A1 Jolson singing "Mammy." He had been an apprentice draftsman with a Philadelphia engineering company. Four years ago to this hour we were flying at 22,000 feet just south of Brunswick. We had just finished an oxygen check, and I had passed the word over the interphone that bandits (enemy fighters) were in the area. Two explosive cannon shells took Bob's life.

I remember seeing the German plane slash across our left wing. I felt the dull shudder of explosive slugs in the back end of the ship, and I knew that we had been badly hit. Together with my co-pilot I feathered an engine mechanically and began to check damage and casualties. The German was a good pilot: he flew so close over our wing that I could see into his cockpit.

Some part of me was aloof from the urgencies of emergency action. I thought how insane it all was. The German was as afraid of the ten fifties mounted on my ship as I was of his own lethal weapons. Even as the bare nerve ends of fear were scraped clean. I knew that no man would choose war of his own accord. Neither of us wished to be up there.

He was a murderer. I was a murderer. It's no use ducking that. Thirty times I carried bombs into Germany and Occupied France. That tonnage would have annihilated that village that we saw in Italy several times over. There is the turn onto the bomb run, several minutes of painstaking subservience to the instruments of science, a faint click, the nose of the plane drops slightly, and bombs are away. Their impact occurs in another world.

On one low-level mission I saw the bombs of the group ahead from the moment they left the planes until impact. It was a tiny hamlet in the Harz Mountains, famous for canaries. There was a man on a bicycle pedaling frantically towards the town as the explosives dropped surely on it from above. The cyclist had just reached town when tiny pin pricks of smoke exploded into mushroom billows of dirty white vapor. Grotesquely enough, I can liken it only to one's childhood imagination of the genie bursting from Aladdin's magic lamp. These were bad genies.

The same rapacious genies have blighted much of Europe. They are concussion, fire, and destruction, with all the consequent evils of famine and hardship that result from the instantaneous descent to chaos that reduces a highly civilized society into brutally primitive surroundings. There do not exist terms fearful enough to impress this truth enough on those who have not experienced or witnessed the desolate wake of modern war.

Take a flight with me low over the cities of Germany from Karlsruhe to Hamburg to Berlin. They are quarries of blasted stone. Each inhabited area seems like a festering scar on the blessedly green surface of the earth. There is a curious drama in the solitary humans, heavily underscored by shadow, who walk along the streets. There is a curious beauty in the tinsel sparkle of pulverized fragments of glass that shine in the sun. There is a curious riddle in the tiny plants that take root in profusion on the bleakest piles.

Or walk with me through some of the Ruhr cities. It matters little which you choose: Essen, Duisburg, Dusseldorf, Cologne. The walls of the homes that once were great stand now like prehistoric ruins. At Cologne even the single bricks are burst apart. Oh, yes. Cologne. They proudly pointed to the still-intact Cathedral of Cologne as evidence of the accuracy of Allied bombing. We spared it, you know, even with the central railroad station and the main bridge over the Rhine only a few hundred yards away. Of course, we demolished all the other buildings in the area, but we spared the Cathedral. Even in war we are merciful. That's why we are different.

I visited Cologne twice at somewhere around 23,000 feet. On the second mission we bombed though the clouds. At that time instrument drops were accurate to within about a half mile of the target. Draw an imaginary circle with a half-mile radius from the point where you are now sitting. How merciful were we? Possibly the survival of Cologne Cathedral was due to the fact that its rib and buttress construction allowed concussion waves to pass through it without doing more than destroying the windows. Possibly it was the sheltering hand of God. I am struck by the coincidence that St. Paul's also has survived in the midst of the leveled acres of Blitzed London.

I visited the Ruhr cities again on a ground trip in May, 1945. We were the conquerors then. We wore steel helmets and carried firearms. We plundered a wine cellar and drove our jeep down the main streets recklessly. Except for an occasional horse-drawn cart there was no German traffic. The few pedestrians who walked on the roads jumped aside quickly as we approached. Our low-level flights had prepared us for the extent of physical destruction. We were not shocked. The Hun had been wicked, and we punished him, even received medals for dealing out the punishment. Who were we to be ashamed of what we had wrought?

The grim desolation was a much greater shock when we returned to Germany this year. More than three years after the end of hostilities there is little evidence of energetic reconstruction. Where three walls were left standing, a fourth has been improvised. Where a foundation had remained intact, it was roofed over. But many sidewalks are still blocked with heaps of brick and mortar. Factory chimneys stand smokeless. You understand the French fear that a rebirth of German energy means a rebirth of predatory nationalism, which has caused 75 years of war with Germany. Yet you know the irreplaceable importance of German industrial and agricultural production to the European economy. You feel that the Germans are enduring only what they deserve. Yet you wonder whether they alone will endure the full measure of penance?

Compared with the wreckage of Germany, destruction in other countries seems less cataclysmic. Yet the smell of urban dismemberment, which is much like that of a rat's nest pulled out of a barn wall by a farmer, hovers over London, Amiens, Florence, and Rotterdam. All of these, and their nations, have suffered wounds like those which were mortal to the deserted village which once stood innocently in that tiny valley in Italy.

Yes. The German is a murderer. I, too, am a murderer. I protest my innocence, and the German would protest his. But we both know that we are guilty. Perhaps it is not more than original sin in man. Are we self-deceived when we cry out with others who suffer that there is a lion in our streets?

–Originally published in Artifacts '48 by The Maple Press Company, York, Pa., 1949.

Bruce was a Captain in the 8th U.S.A.F. as a B-24 pilot. A native of Spring Grove, Pa., he is a graduate of Deerfield Academy, Williams College and Oxford University as a Rhodes Scholar. From 1950 to 1986 he was an English teacher at The Lawrenceville School, Head Master from 1959-1986. He was a founder of the Monadnock Conservancy, served on the boards of several educational organizations and was Moderator of Dublin, N.H., and his church. He and his wife Mary Elizabeth are parents of three children.

Adventure in the Bay of Biscay

Dr. Glyn Millard

In early 1941 I was eighteen years old when I enlisted in the Royal Air Force. I learned to fly as a pilot in Southern Rhodesia, now Zimbabwe, and in South Africa, returning to the United Kingdom via New York City and Halifax, Nova Scotia. I then joined a squadron in northern Scotland performing anti-submarine patrols in the Atlantic, convoys to Murmansk in northern Russia, and later in the Bay of Biscay.

May 30 and 31, 1943 were two significant days in my life, kind of an adventure actually. I spent those two days in a dinghy in the Bay of Biscay after landing in the ocean. We had engine failure in one of our engines. We ditched around eight o'clock in the morning, a Sunday I think, and fortunately it was a beautiful, sunny, calm morning.

Two days before, the famous British film actor, Leslie Howard, who had been flying to Lisbon, Portugal, went missing in this same area. After we ditched, and soon thereafter, there were aircraft visible, but not near. Presumably they were searching for Howard. He was never found, but we were picked up after being in the drink for about 40 hours. The efforts to find him must have helped in our rescue. At least we always thought so.

After being saved by the British Navy, I joined another crew and flew to North Africa, where I joined another squadron in Malta and performed anti-shipping strikes during the Italian Campaign. After completing another tour of operations, I was sent to the Middle East, attended a flying instructor's course, and was posted to Palestine.

Just before the end of the war, I was posted to Athens, Greece, where I met my wife-to-be, Phyllis Keene. She had come to Europe during the war, worked for the United Nations, and opened a nursing college for girls in Athens.

Glyn, from Glamorganshire, South Wales, received his medical education at St. Thomas' Medical School and Massachusetts General Hospital and served as a physician in Peterborough, N.H., for more than 30 years. He and his wife Phyllis had a daughter.

Denmark Under German Occupation

Birgit Faber Morse

On April 9, 1940, German armies and airplanes crossed the Danish-German border, which had been established by plebiscite at the Versailles Treaty in 1920. I remember vividly the waves of low flying planes with the red, black and white painted Nazi swastikas and the noise they made. I was five years old and my little brother just two; he was crying and very scared and thought that they were big birds and they were going to eat him. Everybody in our household seemed subdued and was listening intently to the radio announcements from the Danish government that at the time had a rather neutral political stand against Germany. The Germans tried to assure the Danish population that they came as friends and "Aryan brothers" to protect us against enemies - whoever they would be - but many people believed them.

The Netherlands were occupied about the same time and in similar fashion as Denmark — both flat and low-lying countries were easily overrun. Mountainous Norway, on the other hand, fought the Germans bravely and many Norwegians left the country, including their king. The Danish king, Christian X, stayed in Denmark during the whole war and was a great example for the population by showing his solidarity for the people that the Germans persecuted. As the war progressed and food and other necessities became rationed and scarce, I remember that in Denmark, then primarily an agricultural nation, we never went hungry. Therefore we organized food packages to be sent to both the Netherlands and Norway, where they were starving towards the end of the war.

After the German bombing of London during 1941 and their aborted invasion of Britain, the English, and later the Americans (after Pearl Harbor), joined forces in bombing strategic sites in Germany. Their flight paths went over Denmark, and I have strong memories of air raids, when everybody had to seek shelter or go down into the nearest cellar. At the time we lived in northern Jutland in a big, old, two-story brick house, where my father, a surgeon, had both his office and operating room. During air raids he had mandatory hospital duty. The house had a full basement with room for everybody: family, workers and visitors.

In the beginning of the war the Danes were not very concerned about the air raids, since the German antiaircraft guns could not reach the high flying Allied planes. When they later did we all hurried downstairs, at times even hearing the planes before the sirens. During January and February in 1942, Denmark had a very cold winter and three classmates and I came down with scarlet fever and were interned for over a month in the contagious division of the local hospital. The air raids now came with shorter intervals, but I was not unhappy, since it meant that I saw my father often. When my mother and little brother came to visit they had to stand outside the window in the cold and could only wave to me.

At family dinner on a cold night shortly after I came home from the hospital we suddenly heard a shot ring out. I still remember the whistling sound above my head. The bullet had gone through the window which I was facing and into the wall on the other side of the dining room, where it slightly nicked a picture frame. My parents reported the incident right away to the local authorities and the next day a German officer together with a young soldier with frostbitten hands came into my father's office. They both apologized profoundly and explained that the soldier's mitten became frozen to the gun trigger and that was the reason for the accident.

In 1939 my parents bought a Ford V8 as the family car, but as the war started and everything began to be rationed we could not get enough gasoline to use it regularly. It was therefore stored away up on blocks, but in an emergency it could rapidly come down and be used. Instead my father got permission to buy a small BMW with a generator that could drive on almost anything, including peat moss.

As the war progressed and the Germans' restrictions became more numerous, so did the Danish resistance movement. Weapons from England were parachuted in to the less populated areas in Denmark. They were collected by those in the resistance movement and often hidden in the old animal barns that in earlier days belonged to the country clergy, but now mostly were empty or used for storage.

As the German antiaircraft weapons became more sophisticated, they began to shoot down more Allied airplanes on their way across Denmark to Germany. The resistance movement's network tried to save any survivors coming down by parachute before the Germans could reach them. Here our Ford V8 came in handy, since it could outperform most German cars. Any surviving flier picked up by the resistance was transported out of the area as fast as possible, but they often needed medical attention or temporary accommodation, since the Germans were on the lookout for them.

Late one evening, we first heard a plane overhead, then right away the air-raid siren and shortly thereafter the noise of a plane crashing in the distance. My father took off right away and the rest of us went down into the cellar. I had a cold and was given half a shot of aquavit to help me fall asleep. Later that night a noise in a storage room nearby woke me up. I was in my bed, but feeling better and being rather curious, I got up and went out in the hall to see what was going on. I will always remember what I saw. Two men in dirty and ripped leather suits looked directly at me and said something I did not understand. Right behind them was my father carrying something which looked like a parachute and he sent me a look that made me rapidly disappear into my room. A few minutes later, when things had quieted down, in came Dad and in no uncertain terms told me never to mention to anybody what I saw and heard that night, until the war was over. At this point I had already seen and heard enough to know when to keep my mouth shut.

During the summer of 1943 the Germans began to tighten their control over the Danish population. Most of the police force was interned in camps near the Danish-German border; people of Jewish persuasion had been forewarned and most had left for Sweden, which stayed neutral during the war. The easiest way to escape the country was by small fishing boat motoring across the sound between Denmark and Sweden in the darkness of night. The boats would take off from the coastal area between Copenhagen and Elsinore, where there were many private homes with docks and small harbors. My maternal grandmother had a home on the coast a few miles south of Elsinore, where the whole family usually met each year during the month of July to celebrate her birthday. The summer of 1943 became our last such celebration, since her home and others in similar locations were expropriated by the occupation forces.

On August 29, 1943, the Germans posted proclamations on all houses saying that the Danish government had "resigned" and that the Germans now were in charge of the country. Other restrictions followed - curfew at night and during the day no more than four persons could assemble together outside. I remember it as a beautiful sunny day, and several friends and I decided to go and get ice cream at the local dairy on the way back from school. When we noticed all the posters I do not know what got into us, but we started to pull several of them down and tear them apart. Suddenly a couple of shots rang out, and we were ordered by German soldiers to stop immediately. The four of us took off in different directions. I ran around the corner to close friends of my parents, who took me in and hid me, but they also called my parents to tell them what had happened. A couple of hours later, my father showed up and gave me an earful while looking me over. He noticed that I had dried blood running down my left leg. Apparently I had been hit by a ricocheting bullet, but had not felt anything. After we got home Dad popped a pellet out of the wound and put some disinfecting powder on that stung. Luckily it healed fast without any infection and all I have left of this adventure is a tiny indentation on my leg.

The Germans started early to build large cannon positions (pillboxes) along the west coast of Jutland as anti-aircraft defenses. As the war intensified and they began to fear the invasion of the Allied forces, they spread and reinforced their whole defense system. Beach areas were mined and so were all the sea lanes and fjords surrounding the country. One could not get to the beaches and travelling by boat became dangerous. The Danish resistance movement grew as the war progressed and so did the operations of the Gestapo (secret German police), who in Copenhagen used the expropriated Shell building as headquarters. That same building was also used as a prison for captured resistance fighters. An uncle of mine, who was one of the main organizers of the Resistance movement, unfortunately was wounded and caught in a skirmish with the Gestapo.

They kept him for a week in the prison without medical assistance and finally took him to Ryvangen (burial ground for all Danish resistance people) and shot him. His wife, my mother's younger sister, immediately left for Sweden with my one year old cousin, since she knew so much and was afraid that Gestapo would interrogate her.

Gradually, as I matured and became more aware of the war situation, my parents included me in more of the so called "underground activities." One of my most vivid memories towards the end of the war was sitting with my parents in the cellar at night, secretly listening to the news and messages from BBC. During the last months before the liberation and the German surrender we sat with a map of Europe in front of us. Gradually we drew the lines of the Allied and Russian forces as they progressed towards each other. We all hoped that it would be the Allied forces that would reach Denmark first - and luck had it that this was what happened.

The German surrender came on the eve of May 4, 1945, and Field Marshall Montgomery entered Denmark triumphantly the next day.

Birgit Faber Morse was born and grew up in Denmark through her high school years. She then attended Barnard College in New York City, the University of Copenhagen and graduated from Yale University with an MA in Archaeology. She is still a curatorial affiliate of Yale Peabody Museum and locally a trustee of Historic Harrisville.

THE WAR FROM BEIRUT

PETER OLIVER

My paternal grandparents were British Quaker missionaries who founded an orphanage in the mountains of Lebanon during the early 1900's. My father was born there and, after being sent to the U.S. (at the tender age of seven) for 20 years of school, college, med school and training, returned to the American University of Beirut and its hospital with his American wife. I was born there in 1930.

I remember listening on the radio to the declaration of war against Germany by King George VI in September 1939 - we all stood to attention as "God Save the King" was played. A few months later, Nazi Germany invaded France and the Vichy French were left in control of southern France and Lebanon (which had been their mandate). Dad tried to enlist in the British army, but was told his work in Beirut was more valuable than anything he could do in the service.

During 1940 he was warned that he might be interned by the Vichy, so he and a Canadian doctor at the AUB were taken across the border into Palestine (a British mandate) at night by "professional smugglers" whom my missionary grandfather contacted thru intermediaries! The rest of our family was ferried by the American consul down to Jerusalem where we lived at the American Colony for a month or two.

From Jerusalem, we traveled to Amman, Jordan, and then across the desert to Baghdad where Dad was appointed to the Royal College of Medicine. He performed surgery on little Prince Faisal (who became King Faisal II and was later assassinated in 1958 by his uncle). In his private practice, he used a hospital run by a Jewish nurse for whom he smuggled jewels (sewed to his undershirt because he was never searched at the border) out of Iraq on trips to Lebanon where the Vichy had by now been replaced by the

Free French. He brought out his earnings (in the form of gold coins) in a similar manner to deposit in Lebanese banks. Another missionary was caught driving a car with a solid gold axle out of the country!

Baghdad was surrounded by "bunds" (dikes) to keep the spring floodwaters of the Tigris River from inundating the city. When our cellar was filled to a depth of two feet by the rising water table, the house owner had a couple of truckloads of sand shoveled in resulting in a waterbed floor and low ceiling! We would go downtown in an *arabiya* (horse drawn carriage) with our German shepherd, Ronnie, who was called a *chelb inglesi* (English dog) by the natives. While there, we met a British tank corps commander, Major Renton, who had a Bengal tiger skin with mounted head. The major was later killed in the Western Desert when his tank was disabled and his surrounding corps followed his instructions not to open their turrets in battle.

In the summer of 1941, our family returned to Lebanon without Dad who had a contract to remain in Baghdad for a few more months during which he was interned at the American Embassy by the pro-German government. The son of Field Marshal Kesselring was in Iraq training its air force when he was shot down and killed by an Iraqi firing his rifle in the air (a common way for Arabs to celebrate!). The government asked the natives to confine their approbation to cheers. When Royal Air Force planes bombed the Iraqi air base at Habaniya, Dad and his fellow internees would cheer from the embassy walls until the guards started taking shots at them. Shortly thereafter, Iraq was invaded and conquered by the Brits, so Dad could rejoin his family in Lebanon.

During the following year, Beirut was a R & R (rest and recreation) city for Allied troops fighting the Germans and Italians in North Africa. Mum's contribution to the war effort was to have six to twelve GIs (Brits, Aussies, South Africans and New Zealanders) to our house for "high tea" (with sandwiches, cake and cookies) twice a week. The evening would then progress to a game of Monopoly run by me. Most of the GIs were ones she met on the street (and invited back) plus a regular contingent from the British anti-aircraft battery stationed on the shore below our home. Except for occasional firing practice, the only activity we saw was one night when they opened up with a machine gun firing tracer bullets at what looked like a mine rolling around in the waves. It didn't explode, so must have been an oil barrel. Once, a large group Mum had invited from the army hospital arrived on the wrong day! She valiantly rose to the occasion by buying the whole tray of brioches from a street peddler and dragging me out of school to help.

I was frequently given souvenirs from the campaign - badges and shoulder patches of many regiments (including the Afrikakorps), bayonet, revolver (whose cylinder had been removed to my dismay), shell cases, machine gun belt (filled with live bullets), etc. My riskiest adventure consisted of climbing into a well in the mountains where I had heard some hand grenades had been disposed of. On retrieving one, my first action was to unscrew, by chance, the detonator! Needless to say, I never told my parents about this.

In the summer of 1942, General Rommel was advancing through Libya (Tripoli, Benghazi and Tobruk have become dateline names again) towards the Middle East and a number of families from the AUB decided to try to return to the States. The Mediterranean and Atlantic were closed to civilian ships by U-boats, so the only safe route was via Australia and the Pacific. We took the train to Cairo where we waited a month for a ship. We visited the Sphinx, the Pyramids and numerous museums, but what I enjoyed most was the zoo and its animals. As a ship arrived in Port Said, I was hospitalized at an Italian nuns' hospital with paratyphoid - probably contracted from eating ice cream at the well-known restaurant Groppi's. After my discharge, another ship became available, but we had no information about it - even whether there was a doctor on board. Dad had decided to return to Lebanon, but was unwilling to let me travel without medical coverage, so we all returned with him. Another family took the risk of traveling on the second ship which turned out to be the Queen Mary taking German and Italian war prisoners to Australia for internment. This family, the Dennises, had the top deck to themselves! The Queen was so fast, she didn't need a destroyer escort and entered Sydney harbor at the same time as the preceding ship which had had a week's head start.

Rommel was finally defeated by Montgomery at the battle of El Alamein in September of 1942 which stopped his invasion of the Middle East. Beirut continued to be a R & R city for GI's and Mum kept up her USO activities giving many a welcome taste of home life. After returning from Cairo, I resumed my life as a student at the American Community School which, after the exodus, shrank to about 40-50 pupils. My teen-age sister was enrolled at a British convent school in Jerusalem to protect her from any predatory soldiers! Dad was rationed to one bottle of Haig & Haig each month which he once nobly donated to anointing a haggis which was made for us by a Scottish butcher in the AA battery near us!

In the spring of 1945, the European war was over and we prepared to come to the U.S. In September we embarked from Haifa on the *Gripsholm*, which stopped at Piraeus to pick up Greek, and then at Naples for Italian war brides of American GI's. In the latter port, I can remember shipmates bartering American cigarettes for souvenirs such as Luger pistols.

In the fall of 1945, I resigned myself to the comparatively tame life of an American boarding school.

Born in Beirut, Lebanon, Peter attended the American Community School, the Westtown School, Haverford College and the Boston University School of Medicine. He was an Otolaryngologist at the Lahey Clinic for more than 30 years. He and his wife Connie had three children.

A Gentle Voice on the Battlefield

G. Blake Sabine

I had completed prep school and entered Dartmouth College in 1943 when the Army came to the campus to promote an advanced training plan in engineering, medicine or foreign languages. The offer of a free education seemed too good to pass up.

In June, I joined a group from Harvard which had signed up for the advanced training program. We were sent to a college in Vermont for basic training where we idled the hours away in engineering lore and Army background. After several weeks of such gentle treatment, all the cadets were summoned one day to a parade ground for further instruction. There we were informed that the Army needed us in another capacity, as riflemen for the war in Europe.

We were dispatched to various training camps for Army field training. I went to the 28th Infantry Division where we practiced long marches, digging trenches and firing various weapons. Within four weeks we were on a ship headed across the Atlantic.

We learned how to leave the ship while combat was happening, crawling over the ship's sides on rope lattices to get into a landing boat. Once near enough to France, we waded to the shore with our rifles held high. We either trucked overland or walked, depending on German resistance. We met an occasional flurry of activity from German aircraft and artillery.

My final destination was the 79th (Cross of Lorraine) Division, just past Neufchateau, where they were resting after some hard going from Cherbourg all over central France and Belgium. I was assigned to a scout unit checking for the location of hostile forces. Our orders were to drive the Germans back to Strasbourg on the Rhine River.

The German escape route was wooded rough land, interspersed with open fields and small villages. This made finding small groups of retreating soldiers difficult. In one village we had cleared and taken possession of a large building and barn. A German tank showered us with large-bore shells that had been tampered with by the soldiers so they did not explode. Once the barrage lifted, we found we had stumbled on a German supply food depot. We happily started to dig in until we discovered that they had ruined the food by using the area as a "men's room," so nothing was edible.

We pressed on to another village with better luck. As we entered this town we were greeted by Catholic nuns on the roadside, each flourishing a wine bottle and glass. Even as we were required to march single-file through the village, weapons at alert, we each got refills from the smiling ladies along the entire length of that village.

Another adventure was the night march we quietly carried off in what was supposed to be enemy territory. We were ordered to be totally silent in the dark. As we raced quietly along on the dark trail, we gradually became aware of shrouded figures which appeared from the dark shadows and joined our column. They were German soldiers thinking they were joining a retreat. One of our sergeants in the rear of the column became aware of this problem and started singing out loudly. A decision was made to fall out on the side and let the Germans go by. But when we stopped, they stopped. It turned out that the Germans wanted to surrender, so we collected their weapons and took them to our destination.

From this encounter, I got a wonderful German Luger (which my wife later made me sell). The prisoners turned out to be mostly old men and boys. We met the young soldiers later.

When the enemy took a stand, they counter-attacked with artillery and machine guns. This increased our personnel losses; one of the first was the company commander and his radioman. The next commander sent to us was, unfortunately, a captain taken from antiaircraft command. He had a hasty training in leading foot-soldier units. All went well for several days until we ran into several dug-in machine gun nests on the other side of a flat open field with no discernable cover. The usual procedure would be to call in artillery to dig them out of their holes. The company commander evidently didn't know this because his order was: "Fix bayonets...Charge!"

Our company rose from our generally prone positions and charged across approximately 100 yards. The casualties were high. Many had fairly slight wounds; others were badly injured or killed. I was among the badly injured. I think everyone who was on the attack line that day wondered if they would see tomorrow. I saw my platoon leader go down. He appeared to have leg wounds. The man beside me was next; his injury appeared to be bad — however, he was still conscious. Then I saw the earth in front of me dug up by machine gun bullets and I was hurled to the ground by sudden total impact.

Like any stricken soldier I cried out to God: "Help me, Lord." I heard a voice that instantly replied, "Open your eyes." As I opened my eyes I saw that I had fallen into a depression in the field that protected me from further blasts of machine gunfire or pieces of shell fragments. The gentle voice I heard calmed me completely. I had no doubt that God had answered my cry. I lay out on the ground for about four hours. The gunfire and shelling gradually stopped. I felt completely at ease.

In time two soldiers carrying a litter found me. I was totally helpless, unable to move. They carried me about a quarter mile to the road where a Jeep rigged to carry six litters sat, motor running, but no one near it. I was placed on the Jeep and left to wait. Shortly I found out why no one was present: About a half mile up the road, a large German tank was firing shells at an American tank destroyer which was taking on ammunition as it sat close to the Jeep.

Eventually I arrived at the aid station, where they checked my wounds and sent me to an airfield to huddle on a litter by a fire with fifteen others until dawn, when we were flown to a hospital. We went directly into operating rooms for surgery.

When I awoke I was in a large room with 200-300 men on beds. Soon two men in white coats approached me. They identified themselves as the surgeons who had operated on me. They said their visit was unusual, since they worked every day from dawn to dusk. They had a message for me: I had been hit by two bullets, one into my liver and elsewhere and the other directly through my chest cavity. Theoretically, they said, I should be dead, but I was still breathing and they wondered how that could be. When they had opened my chest they found the right lung had collapsed out of the way of the projectile and it was safely untouched at the bottom of the cavity. They said they weren't believers, but they agreed this was a miracle.

    I spent about four weeks at the hospital. My only memory of that time is the gentle treatment by the nursing and other technical staff. From there I was flown to England for physical conditioning before being sent back to Germany where I served as a medic. The most effective part of my rehabilitation in my view was a tin horn that I was required to try to blow at least four hours a day, an exercise which helped my right lung to expand in my chest and become useful. As I left the rehab unit, the staff said goodbye to me with the cheerful statement that I might live to age 50. (I have enjoyed 85 years to date.)

A native of Brookline, Mass., Blake graduated from Harvard College and worked in sales and marketing throughout his career. He and his wife Thea have one child. Blake also served on his town's planning and school boards and as an elder in his church.

On the Ground with the Third Armored Division

Philip A. Stoddard

In September 1941 I received orders assigning me to duty with the 3rd Armored Division, 18th Ordnance Battalion at Camp Polk, La. I was a very green 24-year-old ROTC Second Lieutenant. What follows are recollections I have treasured for well over fifty years about the colorful and remarkable men that served with me. Battle certainly is not enjoyable, but I prefer to think about the lighter side of soldiering and those who contributed to keeping me "straight." After a period at the Desert Training Center in California, we were stationed for a short time at Camp Pickett, Va. It was there that I was made a Captain and given command of Company A of the Third Armored Division's Maintenance Battalion. We then moved to Fort Indiantown Gap in Pennsylvania where the countryside was pleasing, the people friendly and where there were a number of towns and small cities offering chances for recreation. However, my fondest memory of Pennsylvania was meeting a beautiful young lady who became my bride before I shipped out to England and the battlefields of Europe.

While we were stationed in England getting ready for the Normandy invasion, there were occasions when our drivers had some spare time while the Sherman tanks they had transported were being loaded aboard landing craft. With permission, they took a 2 ½ ton truck to a Red Cross club in a town some miles away where it was "stolen." Speculating that some Navy types had borrowed and abandoned the truck somewhere before shipping out, our crew had to return to home base minus a truck. Obviously the battalion commander was less than pleased and made it clear that the lieutenant in charge would have to pay for it. I tried to plead the lieutenant's case, but the commander made it clear that he expected to see the truck in line when he made his inspection the following Saturday and that we better keep looking.

Master Sergeant Gus and his friends came up with a brilliant idea. They persuaded the ordnance depot officer in charge of "writing off" damaged equipment to let them have a beat-up 2 ½ ton truck which they towed back to our quarters. Working night and day, they rebuilt that truck and at Saturday morning inspection it was there in line with a newly painted correct number and unit markings. That truck was with us when we landed on the beaches of Normandy and I am sure that it performed admirably.

In Europe, our division broke out of the Normandy invasion area and we were confronted on a number of occasions with German defensive positions which had been carefully crafted and were difficult to overcome. When these occurred and high casualties loomed, we called in tactical air support. When the fighter planes arrived, the bombing and strafing helped enormously and were much appreciated by those of us on the ground. The flip side of the coin, however, was the let down we felt at the end of the day when they left to go home. Our troops watched them grouping together, wagging their wings in a good-bye salute and then heading for "home" to what we pictured as a cocktail, a good hot cooked meal and warm dry bed to sleep in. We felt left in the cold, hungry and abandoned.

Our company was a part of Combat Command A, which made good progress across France. Our mission was to bring up the rear of the task force and do what we could to repair and quickly return to service any tanks, self-propelled artillery and any other ordnance that had fallen out of line.

On one occasion, our line of march came to a fork in the road some miles from the starting point. A crew from our company had fallen behind to assist a broken-down tank. Unable to fix the tank, they tried to catch up but took the wrong fork in that road and ran into a German formation and were taken prisoner. The Germans were in retreat mode and in some disorder. Our men were therefore able to escape during the night and find their way to an American unit. It turned out the hero of that group was Private Fraunfelter.

He was a qualified and able young soldier, a real asset to our battalion, but found himself in real difficulty with the local constabulary when he became involved in a fracas with a civilian while we were stationed in Pennsylvania. He faced some jail time and we faced the loss of a good man. I finally was able to persuade the locals to let the military handle the situation. The decision to save Fraunfelter was validated when every one of the group that escaped from the Germans agreed that the private had been their leader. He kept them together and did the planning.

It was not unusual for some of the troops to get into disciplinary problems and get demoted. I believed that they were willing and able soldiers and should not be dismissed merely as "grunts." I have vivid and fond memories of one particular person who became very important to me. I could write a book about him.

August W. (Gus) Snickars was Master Sergeant of Company A with 29 years of service, beginning in World War I. Gus was a stocky, interesting, dependable, wise and loyal man; the quintessential "old soldier." He had served many years in an Army that was small, underfunded and not largely noticed. They did not have the amenities that we "modern" soldiers had but they were canny, resourceful, hard drinking and took their pleasure where they found it.

It is axiomatic that sergeants run the Army on a day-to-day basis. We will never know how many "wet behind the ears" officers Gus educated and guided over the years. By the manner of being addressed, officers could tell when they finally were accepted by the old timers. "When would the Lieutenant like it done?" changed to "When would you like it done, sir?" This, coupled with the crispness of a salute, let you know where you stood.

Gus would never see a doctor voluntarily. He suffered colds, arthritis, bumps and bruises stoically because he feared his various ailments and age might preclude his being sent overseas. He wanted to be part of the action. Gus had been really worried about the final physical before shipping out. Fearing he might not pass the exam, he dieted and temporarily gave up his beer. On the day of the exam, we were ushered into a cavernous room and ordered to step in and out of a disinfecting foot bath. It turned out that was almost the extent of the "physical." Gus passed and in celebration got tolerably drunk.

An Armored Division doesn't "march" in the usual sense. Everyone rides in a vehicle: a tank, half-track, truck or jeep. Gus rode with my driver and me in my jeep. He was having some trouble seeing as well as he wanted to and was using a pair of cheap magnifying glasses. Before the break-out in Normandy, enemy and animal dead were lying along the roadside. As we went along, Gus spotted a bespectacled German corpse and asked us to stop while he relieved it of its glasses. I know this happened more than once until he found a pair that he felt were better than his own.

Our combat unit was coiled for the night during a particularly chaotic period when the Germans were trying to escape encirclement in Belgium. Repair efforts were hectic as well. In the middle of things, a captured German sedan was being used by one of our units but it had a broken spring. Obviously spare parts were not available. Gus went over to the periphery and brought back a sapling. He cut it to length, fitted and fastened it to the old spring and the car was back in business.

When we crossed into Germany, things were different. There were no friendly faces and no signs of welcome. One evening we were dining on K or C rations and Gus disappeared for a few minutes. He returned with a dozen fresh eggs which he had "requisitioned" from a farm nearby. We were not supposed to do this kind of pilfering in France and Belgium but in Germany we felt it more than justified. Having finished the first dozen eggs, there was agreement that an "encore" was in order. However, the farmer had apparently seen the heist and put a padlock on the henhouse. Poor Gus was not happy. He returned and put one of our spare padlocks on the door saying if we couldn't have a few eggs, the "Kraut" was not going to have any either. I later was told by an old friend of mine that an infantry unit would have blasted the lock open with a .45, helped themselves and then dealt with the inhospitable treatment with a couple of hand grenades.

The Division had just broken through the Siegfried Line into Germany and was stopped for a few days to repair and refit. Occupying a cement plant on the outskirts of town provided us with a "hard stand" that would keep us out of the mud and facilitate our work. We had just settled in when an artillery captain arrived indicating this was an ideal spot for his purpose and he really needed the space. I reluctantly agreed to make room and moved our unit to the end of the complex. The captain set up his battery and began intermittent harassing fire. The enemy, of course, returned fire trying to locate him. As a result, we were getting "incoming mail" rather frequently. In the meantime, for a safe place to sleep, Gus commandeered a small flat-roofed scale house. To enhance its safety, he recruited one of our ten-ton wreckers to carry a sheet of boiler plate which he had located and install it on the roof of his "home away from home." It had not taken him long to locate and install his security blanket. It was just another example of the ingenuity and resourcefulness of this old soldier.

Somewhere along the line, word came down that we should consider promoting senior non-commissioned officers to the rank of Warrant Officer. Such promotions recognized top leadership and skill and took them into officer ranks in most respects. Although under a lot of pressure from the Colonel to accept, Gus respectfully declined the opportunity. He reasoned that he would not be comfortable fraternizing with officer types after almost 30 years as an enlisted man. All of us felt that he would have been a great Warrant Officer but respected his decision.

Gus told me that after the war, "he was going to retire to Kentucky, marry "Louisville Lou" and drink himself to death.

Because the name 3rd Armored and 3rd Army is similar, General Patton received a lot of publicity that really belonged to the 3rd Armored Division. Ripley's Believe It Or Not had this to say about the 3rd Armored Division:

First to fire a shell in Germany
First to breach the Siegfried line
First to cross the German border since Napolean
First to capture a German town
First to shoot down a plane from German soil
Greatest one-day advance in history of mobile warfare-
    101 miles

And so, with Gus and many others like him, we won the war. But our victory was costly. In the 3rd Armored Division alone there were 2,126 killed and 6,963 wounded. I was lucky and my recollections are more about my men than they are about me. Rough and tumble as they were, they taught me a lot and I will always remember them.

Several years after the war was over, I was in Louisville and thought of Gus. I was able to track him down and we had dinner at his home. I do not know what I expected his "Louisville Lou" to look like, but she turned out to be an attractive, pleasant and motherly type. Her real name was Ruth and she obviously adored Gus. We had a wonderful reunion.

Born in Hingham, Mass., Philip attended the Massachusetts Institute of Technology and worked for that university in administration throughout his career, retiring as a vice president in 1980. He and his wife Lucille have two children.

From Flight Training to Radio Repair

Richard Swahnberg

After graduating from Keene High School in 1941, I decided to learn how to to fly. I went to Georgia to train as a pilot with the goal of becoming a commercial pilot. I was in training when Pearl Harbor occurred.

At that time, the U.S. Army Air Corps required two years of college and the minimum age to join up was 20. The Royal Canadian Air Force, however, would take an eighteen-year-old for flight training. A friend and I went up to Montreal and enlisted in the R.C.A.F., along with many other Americans. For the next few months, we trainees were marched around and given various kinds of instruction preparing us for flight school. In March 1942, the U.S. Army Air Force dropped its eligibility age to 18, and the R.C.A.F. allowed the U. S. citizens in its ranks to transfer to the U.S. Army if they wished.

In July 1942, a group of us was discharged from the R.C.A.F. and we returned to the U.S. to await further orders. While waiting, I was at home in Keene, and my father put me to work at Kingsbury until December 1942, when I was ordered to report for duty.

My first duty was basic training at Atlantic City, N.J., then at the Nashville, Tenn., Classification Center where I was selected to go to college and then Officer Candidate School. I was sent to Colorado State College to study engineering. After two terms, and anticipating D-Day, the Army closed down the college program and, in March 1944, I was sent to Fort Leonard Wood [Missouri] for infantry training. However, after D-Day, June 6, 1944, I was sent to Fort Monmouth, N.J. to become a radio technician on FM and AM equipment. The Army had discovered that FM radio worked better in combat conditions than the AM band, which the Germans were using.

In September 1944, I married Jini Hanrahan and we had but a weekend pass for our honeymoon. Further training took me to the Lexington, Ky., Signal Depot and then to Fort Jackson S.C., to prepare for deployment to Europe, which occurred in February 1945.

The ship we sailed on was an old United Fruit Company "banana boat" which, at 6 knots, was the slowest in the convoy. After 17 days the ship arrived at Cardiff, Wales, and my group eventually went to Winchester, England, and then to Le Havre, France.

The U. S. Army crossed the Rhine at Remagen, March 3, 1945. Their units worked their way to Aachen and then into Germany to Mönchengladbach.

The radio repair teams were organized into eight-man groups with a cargo truck, a shop truck and a generator trailer. One of our assignments was to salvage radio equipment from tanks that had been damaged during the battles nearby, including the Bulge. It was gruesome work.

The next move was south to Nuremberg where the Company HQ was in a factory building near the stadium, which was used as a large gasoline depot. I was there when the war in Europe ended, May 8, 1945.

The Army detailed several units to scour the countryside between Nuremberg and Dresden, which had been devastated, to seize German war material before the Russians arrived. It was during this time that I discovered that cigarettes were more acceptable than money with the local populace!

The search for material took some weeks and then our unit went to Rheims and on to Nice for some R&R. We expected to be redeployed to the Far East and Japan from Marseilles, but when the war ended in August, our unit boarded a ship, the U.S. Navy transport *Sea Tiger*, sailed past Gibraltar and then turned northwest toward the U.S., reaching Newport News, Va., on September 1, 1945.

I was sent first to Camp Campbell, Ky., and then home on a 45-day furlough and then to Fort Knox Ky.,, where I was discharged on December 26, 1945.

Some years later, while I was working at Kingsbury Corporation, I completed my flight training at the Keene airport and became a private pilot. I became head of a flying club, the "Wingkings" and flew around the New England states on business and pleasure.

After growing up in Keene, N.H., Richard attended the University of New Hampshire and worked as a sales engineer and advertising manager at the Kingsbury Corp. He is a longtime member of the Lions Club and has supported many civic and charitable organizations. He and his wife Virginia had four children.

THE WAR FROM BERLIN

KARIN VAN STRIEN

In the summer of 1939 our family spent the summer vacation in sunny Austria ... the last happy time our family vacationed together. World War II started September 1, 1939. The Blitzkrieg in Poland lasted only a few days. We were told that Germans had been persecuted there.

One has no idea what "war" is like. My father, a WWI veteran, did not talk much about it.

But I remember one day when he took me and my brother for a stroll through the streets and the question of "war" came up. Usually very positive and optimistic, this time my father was rather serious, saying some ominous words of what might come; I do not remember exactly the entire content, but remember that I felt like shivering.

We already had prepared for the days to come. The first impact came with the "blackout" (*Verdunkelung*). Every home had to be completely arranged inside so that no speck of light could shine through to the street. People watched each other's windows very carefully and everybody obliged.

Next came the cleaning of the attic which had been used as storage rooms for tenants. Everything had to be removed, the compartment partitions, furniture, etc. Most of it was sold, because our cellar would become now our second home for the many nights we had to sit there during the unending air raids. Heaps of sand now covered the empty space of the attic. This came in very handy for our air raid warden (*Luftschutzwart*) who would inspect the attic during the raid and, if necessary, would throw the incinerating phosphor bombs out the window onto the lawn in front of the apartment complex before they could do more damage. People who had left their homes in Berlin for the country with nobody left to do this lost their homes from fire. My girlfriend's mother made regular inspections of their attic with a cooking pot on her head, for protection.

Of course, if a blockbuster (*Sprengbombe*) or a mine hit your house you would be done for. In one apartment complex, Handel Platz, people were buried alive. They gave knocking sounds for three days, but nobody could help them; there were just too many demolished houses and not enough equipment to deal with them all. When our immediate neighborhood was hit heavily, the walls of our apartment received big cracks which remained there for many years to come, and the windows shattered. People became very efficient in fixing broken windows in one way or the other.

The bombing of Berlin started in 1940 and continued to the end of the war in 1945. I might mention that of all the bombs the Germans dropped on England during the entire war, their equivalent was dropped in one night in Berlin. Air raids became a way of life. When the radio mentioned that enemy planes were approaching Hannover and Braunschweig, we Berliners knew that meant they would come to us.

How I hated the howling of the sirens, close by and very loud. It signified "Flieger Alarm." To reach our cellar we had to leave our apartment for a short walk outside, down the stairs to the cellar that was shared by the entire apartment complex. The cellar was on the same level with the street, not very protective. There, we would have to wait till the danger was over, signaled by the long, single sound of the siren (*Entwarnung*). We went back to our beds; sometimes we had our sleep interrupted two or three times in one night.

In the early years of the war, only the British planes came to Germany at night, especially during a bright moonlight night. The American planes joined them later during the day.

Sometimes it was a long wait in the cellar and we would take our homework with us. What was it like to go and be in the cellar? When an alarm came at suppertime we would have to leave everything on the table and go. I tried to snitch a bite quickly of what was there, never knowing what would happen. The anxiety was obviously present. My mother always had to visit the bathroom. The cellar filled up with the other people and everybody got quiet. It was ominous to hear the planes flying, and wondering if a bomb would hit us. A feeling of total helplessness. We could not defend ourselves, dependent on the second the bomb was released and where it would go. Why did they do this to us? What had we done to them? We, here in this cellar. We just had to wait and to take it. Not a very good situation. Everybody seemed to have the same thought ... God help us and spare us ... not realizing that if God spared us, what about the others who were not so lucky? One can be really selfish. The anxious moments passed, and life went on. What a relief to hear the long, single sound of the all-clear alarm.

One event in the summer of 1940 remains vividly in my memory: the return of our troops from the short victorious offensive in France. Smiling and sunburned, they marched along the famous Unter den Linden street in the center of Berlin, and we were there joyously to shower them with flowers. This scene would never happen again.

Theatre in Berlin was still thriving. We saw some wonderful performances. I took dancing lessons with my girlfriends in a dance studio at the Kurfuerstendamm (no rock and roll!). One of the boys' parents gave a lovely party in their spacious home; "Bluemchen" was the best waltz dancer. We also liked fox-trot, swing and the "Lambeth - walk." Bluemchen, too, was killed in the war. Letters sent to boys on the front often came back with a notation: "Fallen for Great Germany."

The government decided then to start with a project (*Kinderlandverschickung*) to evacuate children from Berlin's bombing raids to small, safe villages in Austria. Many private homes and hotels were occupied for this purpose. The children attended school in the morning with their teachers, while we older teenagers occupied them in the afternoon. The children, however, got really upset when they heard on the radio of air raids over Berlin, worrying about their loved ones. The safety of being away from the bombs did not make them feel better. Scarlet fever broke out in one of the residences and we had to return home to school. We had already missed a lot of school in 1941. A year later (1942) school classes were asked to help the farmers in East and West Prussia. Three of us girls were assigned to a county in East Prussia, a beautiful fertile countryside, now ethnically cleansed of Germans, and in Russian and Polish hands. For me it meant working in the fields, loading wagons with sheaves of grain, watching and milking cows. I got pretty good at the latter. We were milking right in the meadow, where cows and horses grazed together; we just put a little stool under the cow. One time a lusty horse came galloping towards the cows, at which point my cow, Ella, got afraid, gave my pail a kick with her hoof, and ran away; the wonderful milk spilled into the grass.

I came back to school for a while, until "coal-vacation" started, because of lack of coal to heat the school. Earlier, the authorities had tried to save on heat by closing the boys' school nearby (my brother's) and move the boys into our girls' Lyceum for the morning session; we girls attended the afternoon session. Our teachers told us that there were a lot of "memos" removed from the empty inkwells before we girls could enter the class! We also took turns in air raid service for the school, carrying a gas mask with us.

The early days of March 1943 were designated for our final exams (*Abitur*). But they had to be postponed because several of our classmates in our class of 15 girls were bombed out and lost their homes. Just around this time, one early morning, my mother's sister and her husband came crying to our four-room apartment; they had just lost their beautiful spacious apartment on the 4th floor in Schoeneberg. They had recently inherited elegant antique furniture, paintings, fancy china, carpets, from my aunt's mother-in-law in Munich. It was a terrible shock to them and us. They found shelter and comfort in our home, until they could relocate.

Since the bombing did not seem to have the desired effect on us civilians, the British Air Marshal Harris (we call him "Bomber Harris") tried now to "smash Germany to its knees," starting in spring with the Battle of the Ruhr, trying to wipe out the industrial heartland. However, the production never ceased, but some of the towns suffered badly, including Cologne, Frankfurt, Mainz and others. In the summer of 1943, Hamburg was bombed, causing the famous firestorm where thousands of people burned to death in the flames (at least 80,000 perished, so I heard). Bomber Harris also targeted Berlin, and our nice southwestern suburbs suffered heavy damage. Several of my classmates were at that time bombed out, especially on August 26, 1943.

April 1943 brought changes in our family: my father left for Russia and I left home after graduating from Lyceum to do my obligatory duty for my country - a half year of work service (*Arbeitsdienst*) to help the farmers north of Berlin and a half year of war service (*Kriegshilfadienst*) which I did on the trolley in Berlin. We had the choice of working as a nurse, which was all filled up, in a munitions factory or on the trolley.

A few days after arriving at camp I received a telephone call from my mother that my brother was missing in action in Tunisia, Africa. Another shock, another time for tears to relieve the pain. I remember that another girl, whom I had befriended on the train riding to the camp, and I went into a broom closet and we cried together. Unfortunately she later got sick and had to be released from the camp; she could, however, still share my joy when the news came that my brother was alive and a POW until 1948.

During the summer of 1943, my cousin Jochen, who had been fighting the guerillas in Poland, was wounded and hospitalized in the outskirts of Berlin. When I visited him there, he introduced me to one of his friends who had lost both arms, learning to write with a certain device on his arm-stump. Despite his affliction, he was laughing, joking, and smiling. It was such a sad sight. I admired his courage. My cousin's wound in his knee was open and draining for the rest of his life.

Our work consisted mostly of helping in the fields, weeding endless rows of sugar-beets, harvesting potatoes, etc. We worked with Polish and Russian prisoners together. I remember the beautiful Russian songs of one prisoner as he emptied our potato wickerbaskets into the wagon.

One evening, August 23, 1945, we could watch from our camp heavy air traffic towards Berlin with green and red "Christmas trees" flares in the sky. We heard that my suburb (Steglitz) was heavily hit. The Berliners had been warned beforehand and many had left for the country, including my mother and grandmother. I wanted to see for myself what happened and found a way to get there under the excuse of needing to purchase some necessities for our camp. What a relief to see that our apartment complex was still standing, thanks to our efficient warden. But how awful it looked around us, burned-out ruins everywhere. The church and parsonage beside us destroyed, entire streets completely in rubble. I climbed through our window into the apartment, having the urge to take something back with me. I chose some photographs, and the rosary with a one-inch crucifix at its end from a wooden sculpture of a Catholic saint. I wondered why I, a Protestant, not believing in superstition, would do something like that. Strange things happen in times of turmoil.

The worst air raids I experienced came at the time I served my war duty on the trolley in Berlin. Bomber Harris started "The Battle of Berlin" on November 18, 1943, with a relentless attack that continued until March 1944. More than one thousand planes, each dropping between 1,000 to 2,000 tons of bombs, were involved in the 24 sorties against the German capital. The city continued to be bombed intermittently until the end of the war.

Our camp, located in Lichtenberg, the eastern part of Berlin, was a former dancing hall with a huge chandelier in the middle of the hall, surrounded by bunkbeds for us "war service maidens." Because of the shortage of men workers, who served as soldiers on the front, we were trained to take their place, 10 hours a day, starting at 4 a.m. We learned how to handle several types of trolley tickets to be punched for time, place, directions, etc; how to carry the electrical device at the end of the line around to be placed into the electrical wires above, etc.

Right after my training I came down with yellow jaundice, probably transmitted by a fleabite that got infected. I was supposed to go into the military hospital in the center of the city, but my mother fought and insisted that she would care for me at home. This was lucky, because the hospital was heavily damaged in the bombing, with large numbers of patients killed. At home we again provided refuge to our woman doctor and her husband who were bombed out and stayed with us until they found other quarters. (Later our apartment was reduced to just two rooms because of housing shortage.)

After three weeks recuperation, I had to be back on the trolley for a 10-hour work day. We drove all over Berlin; the trolleys had no doors and the driver had to stand up in front. When alarm sirens howled, we had to race through the rubble-covered streets to find a bunker or cellar. Here, you sit in a strange cellar for long, anxious moments. You hear the noisy, violent crashes nearby, dust coming through the door, so that you clutch your briefcase closer to your body. Some days, when it was quiet on the trolley, I took my little booklet of poems by Hoelderlin out, to divert myself into a more beautiful world. After one of those terrible air raids, which destroyed the church in Lichtenberg, our dancing hall "with parquet floor" was damaged, the huge chandelier lying broken on the floor.

When it was announced that our camp was to be closed because of an infestation of rats, I asked for a transfer closer to home, as my free time was mostly spent on trains to and from home. Based in Zehlendorf, my friends could visit me on my trolley, help me to pull the strings to signal the driver. At least we had some fun. One of them, a law student who was deferred from military service, was later killed by a Russian when the Russians occupied the city. The other, who already had lost an arm in the war, died a year later of infection on his stump.

During another heavy air raid, we ended up hiding in a subway station. Never again, I thought, because the noise level of the bomb explosions amplified there and made it seem worse. When we came out, Baerbel and I were warned to be careful and watch for phosphor spilled by the incinerating bombs on the streets. We ran as fast as we could; and when our feet got hot, we stopped to see if the phosphor had crept through our soles. We were safe!

Another time, during an American air raid in bright daylight, we took shelter in a bunker full of mothers and crying children. I was standing in the entrance, clutching the person next to me, when the air pressure threw me from one corner to the other. A huge bomb had just missed our bunker landing just to the side of it, creating the biggest crater I ever saw in my life. Many more of these craters pockmarked the street and surrounding area. One had burst a water pipe, the water spilling down all over the street. And we found our poor trolley a burned out skeleton. I ran towards home, seeing people sitting in front of their now smoldering houses clutching some of the things they could salvage. It was a sad sight. I think I cried all the way home, running to a telephone to see if my family had survived. They did.

Since many trolleys were out of commission we had to work on double-decker omnibuses, with one girl upstairs and one girl downstairs. I took the upstairs, which was for smokers. We served the city's most populated sections, Friedrich Wilhelm Platz to the Zoo, back and forth for little money. I felt sorry for the exhausted, haggard people who had to jam into the vehicle. Sometimes I felt like a mother-hen who had to take care of them.

After another assault during the night on February 15, 1944 by British and American bombers, word came that Steglitz was badly hit again. I could not help it, but sneaked out of the camp, not thinking of the consequences, trying to find out what happened to my family. I hitched a ride with a jeep filled with soldiers, which brought me a good stretch forward to the Steglitz town hall. From there the usual way is down Albrecht street, a long commercial street with shops downstairs, and four to five floors of apartments upstairs. I was aghast at what I saw. The entire street was a burning inferno, the houses on both sides of the street were all burning, flames shooting out from top to bottom.

I tried to get through, but it was impossible. After a long detour with burning houses everywhere, I finally reached home. When I saw that everything was dark and safe, I fell on my knees with a thankful heart. My grandmother opened the door, telling me that my parents were helping at the neighboring house, forming a water-pail chain till up to the burning attic. I helped for a while, but then remembered my unauthorized leave. Hurrying back to the camp through the still-simmering, smoldering Albrect street, with sparks flying through the air, I fastened my kerchief tighter over my hair. In the morning I got just a warning for my transgression. The camp leader seemed to understand.

Talking with my colleagues, by that time we anticipated that the war was lost, as the Russians were moving closer to our borders. Of course, Churchill insisted on "unconditional surrender." After my war duty was finished in Spring 1944, I moved to a school in Bavaria, while my parents insisted on staying in Berlin.

I came home in December 1944 for Christmas vacation and took one of the last regular trains out of Berlin to Munich at the end of January 1945. Across from me in my compartment was sitting a young family with two small children, one of them a baby: refugees from the East, now all coming to escape the Russian onslaught; they could take along only what they could carry, and that was some bedding and the children. The mother tried desperately to heat a baby bottle over a candle, and was greatly relieved when, at the next station, the women of the "station mission" (*Bahnhofsmission*) helped her with baby food, and supplies. The family wanted to seek refuge with relatives in Nuernberg, which also was targeted by numerous air raids. I wondered sometimes if they survived. We heard about the most cruel bombing of Dresden in February 1945, in which my classmate's parents and brother perished. They had been bombed out in Berlin and thought they were safe in Dresden. And Bomber Harris now has a statue in London!

It was not until the summer of 1948 that our family could be together again, when my brother, released as an English POW, returned from Egypt. The short reunion was interrupted by the start of the Berlin blockade. And that is another story.

Some final comments about Berlin: Most of Berlin's buildings were reduced to rubble after the war was over; tens of thousands civilians were killed or maimed; 1.5 million made homeless. But, most of Berlin's war industry continued. The population's morale was never broken. The British historian Max Hastings summed it up: "In the operational sense the Battle of Berlin was more than a failure. It was a defeat. ... Berlin won. It was just too tough a nut to crack." ("Bomber Command," London : Michael Joseph, 1979)

My conclusion:

War is obsolete.

"Area" (saturation) bombing of civilians, wherever it occurs, is a crime.

Two wrongs do not make a right.

Born in Thuringia, Karin lived in Berlin from 1930 on. She graduated from the Girls Lyceum in Berlin and later earned a Masters from Boston University's School of Social Work and worked in psychoanalytic counseling. She was also a minister's wife for more than 30 years.

Letters to the Homefront

Roger B. Wilson

June 23, 1943
Fort Devens, Mass.

Dear Mother:

"Processing" is over today, and the pressure really went off. I spent the morning on WAAC detail, cutting a blade of grass occasionally but watching the gals train most of the time. This afternoon I helped lay out a softball diamond with a couple of the "ponies" (girls). I rather like this way of fighting. So far I have avoided KP which is extremely important. Food: plentiful, good but rammed down. Sleep: too damn little. Officers: some good, but the lower they are in rank, the more "cheap" they hand out.

Love, Roger

June 25, 1943
Fort Devens, Mass.
Dear Dad:

So far this army has been fairly satisfactory. Yesterday I hit the jackpot and was put on guide duty, marching the new fellows around. I could step to the front of any mess line, took no "cheap" from anyone and gave orders to the boys when necessary. To show how lucky I've been, my friend, Wendy, was on two 16-hour days of KP. None for me so far! We should head west soon.

Love, Roger

June 27, 1943
Camp Hale, Pando, Colo.
Dear Grandmother:

By employing all of my natural charm, plus a few dirty tricks here and there, I have arrived at my destination well rested and quite pleased with the army so far. The biggest change from Devens is the appearance of the soldiers, all tan, rugged looking young fellows. Today we marched about seven miles up into a pass. I felt the altitude only a little. I think I shall like it very much here.

Love, Roger

July 6, 1943
Camp Hale, Pando, Colo.
Dear Mother:

I am rushing like mad as I have just been issued an M1 Garand [rifle], and it requires exhaustive cleaning due to the oil it came in. Last Saturday I really felt the altitude at 12,000 feet. Several of the recruits were snapped right into the hospital, and a forced march took a good toll even of the old timers. Food is poor, little or no butter or sugar, beans, potatoes, and rolls all the time and daily frankfurts. I don't mind though.

Love, Roger

July 15, 1943
Camp Hale, Pando, Colo.
Dear Mother:

I started sharpshooter training with a "22." The best fun is rapid fire, nine shots in 53 seconds from different positions. The old gun kicks quite a bit, but the amazing thing is the ease with which you can shoot bulls at 500 yards when the target is barely visible. The prospects for advancement are slim. I should have gone somewhere else if I wanted to have any bars. This week I have been squad leader, but I still manage to give orders on the wrong foot altogether too often. I have qualified with both the Garand and the Browning machine gun. Today I started grenades. That leaves only the automatic rifle, mortar and .45 pistol.

Your reports of parties at the Ritz and fishing in Vermont made me damn Hitler and Tojo even more. Next week we are going on bivouac at high altitude for two weeks.

Love, Roger

Sept. 12, 1943
Camp Hale, Pando, Colo.
Dear Dad:

I am trying to transfer to the Air Corps. They have opportunities for commissions, and you get real training instead of learning how to march month in and month out. So, could you get me three letters of recommendation? The usual thing, perhaps impressive letter paper is all that is necessary!

Love, Roger

Sept. 24, 1943
Camp Hale, Pando, Colo.
Dear Mother:

Thanks for sending out my birth certificate. So many fellows are trying to get out of here through the Air Corps that I am afraid they may put a stop to transfers. Our best sergeant went last week. If I don't get out, there may be a chance of a promotion because of those vacancies. We were on bivouac last week, and I thought it a privilege to be allowed to sleep until six o'clock. I now appreciate the old saying "stubborn as a mule" as I watch those miserable critters raising hell around camp and received instructions on loading and packing them properly. What independent beasts they are! N.C.O. bivouac tomorrow in wet snow at 11,000 ft. promises to be grim in the mornings, so a little sleep is in order now.

Love, Roger

Nov. 1, 1943
Camp Hale, Pando, Colo.
Dear Mother:

Our division has just been on our first large-scale maneuver. For my part, I had the misfortune of tangling with mules which carried my machine guns and found myself no match for a mule on a steep, slippery, log-barricaded upgrade. The steeper it is the faster the damn things climb, and I usually operate just the other way. But, when it comes to going downhill, the miserable beasts refuse to move if the hill is steep and rocky which forces one to practically drag them from below. One boy barely dodged a somersaulting mule while going through that routine. I am going to machine gun school again. I will be probably reviewing the nomenclature of the M19184A from now on ad infinitum or at least until the war is over and I have missed it.

Love, Roger

Jan. 11, 1944
Jefferson Barracks, Mo.
Dear Mother:

My last day in the field was enough to bring forth a prayer or two. The mercury quotations were from 24° to 35° below. Faces and feet froze right and left, the snow jeeps (weasels) broke down, and we had coffee and beans at 2:30 followed by a blizzard. I was called back because my Air Corps assignment came through. When I told the Colonel I was leaving, he said, "Jesus Christ!" The Major said nothing. I will be there for about a month of basic training (Here I go again.) Know anyone in St Louis?

Love, Roger

Jan. 20, 1944
Jefferson Barracks, Mo.
Dear Mother and Dad:

It hurts plenty to write that you have a son who is a failure, perhaps more because I have never failed at anything before. The first day of the Cadet exams was a six-hour test under the heading of "Psychological." The next day was a test on coordination with all sorts of mechanical and electrical apparatus, peg tests, etc.; the 3rd and 4th days were the G4 physical plus an interview with a psychiatrist. At the final check desk, the Major said, "Disqualified, psychological." And that is all I know.

Maybe it will do me some good to fold at something, but I am mighty disappointed. I guess I'll get sent to gunnery or radio school and may get on a bomber. Anyway, better than Camp Hale, something new, and maybe some flying. Sorry about folding.

Love, Roger

Feb. 2, 1944
Jefferson Barracks, Mo.
Dear Dad:

Last night we were yanked out of bed at 10 for a clothing check, went back to bed at about 11:30 and were pulled out again at 3:30 to stand in a cold rain until about 6. I picked up a cold which will be a good excuse to do a little bunk fatigue. I never did much "gold- bricking" at Camp Hale, but I am proud to say that a good friend of mine and I are competing for the Squadron B championship!

Love, Roger

Feb. 11, 1944
Sioux Falls, S. Dak.
Dear Mother and Dad:

What have I ever done to deserve exile to this wilderness? With all the nice places I might have gone, I have the good fortune to be sent to South Dakota in the midst of a mid-western blizzard that would rival Camp Hale's best. Please, Mother, do you know anyone in the Sioux Falls area (maybe an old Smith friend) by any miracle?

Love, Roger

Feb. 19, 1944
Sioux Falls, S. Dak.
Dear Mother:

This is a school for radio gunners and lasts five months. The base is small, mostly washed-out cadets who wish they were somewhere else. I would transfer to the Coast Guard if I wasn't an inch too short! I have done very little here. One day we moved 3,000 beds, plus four or five truckloads of folding cots and about 1,500 foot lockers from one warehouse to an identical one across the street. I think that if things go according to schedule we will move them back next week. However, the food is good, the company fair, and we get to sleep until 6:45. Life is pretty good.

Love, Roger

March 2, 1944
Sioux Falls, S. Dak.
Dear Grandmother:

    My first class is code over earphones, and it comes very fast. An hour and a half of "dits" and "dats" is fairly nerve-wracking. Then I go to radio theory and then to code again. If I can only finish and get on a B-29! Mother would like it here because they have soy beans or soy bean soup almost every day. I like them very much too.

Love, Roger

April 26, 1944
Sioux Falls, S. Dak.
Dear Dad:

    In answer to your note on my army career, it's not that I give a damn about the prestige of being an officer or about what people will think when the war is over, but all this time wasted is what gets me down. It is nearly a year now since I left for Fort Devens. By the time I get back, I will be three years out of Harvard, know less than I did then and have never had a chance to try myself in any kind of a responsible position. The war may be over sooner than we thought, and I will have done a lot of training while other boys have done my fighting. Ike has my go-ahead! My ears are glued to the radio waiting for the big push.

Love, Roger

June 18, 1944
Sioux Falls, S. Dak.
Dear Grandmother:

    I have been working with some complicated radio sets, never saw so many dials. I get all sorts of shortwave stations, including "Your Hit Parade" in Spanish (until the instructor catches me). I have not yet passed "blinkers," things to which I seem to be rather blind, but I think I will graduate anyway. There should be another stripe if all goes well. Mother's Smith friends have entertained me royally!

Love, Roger

July 22, 1944
Sioux Falls, S. Dak.
Dear Mother:

    I want to summarize my army experience as a great waste of time. In Fort Devens, the army was novel, and I was determined to see what kind of a soldier I could make of myself. I felt good to be in uniform at last as most of my friends had been in the fight for a long time. The trip west to the Tenth Mountain Division was exciting with my first views of the mountains, but that novelty was soon offset by the drudgery and waste of good time which made up infantry life. I am glad I made the move from that windswept hole to the Air Corps even though I didn't make cadets. I am still unable to pass "blinkers" and may "wash back" again. (Compensating factor: a Colonel's daughter has a strange idea that I may be doing this for her, and I don't think she should be disillusioned!)

                                                                     Love, Roger

August 5, 1944
Yuma, Ariz.
Dear Mother:

    Since my last letter, I passed my tests, "washed ahead" one week, flew once, managed evening passes, wound up my business in Sioux Falls (Colonel's daughter included), graduated, shoveled coal for a couple of days and jumped a train for the desert. The troop train, naturally, started out for Arizona by going 200 miles east to Des Moines. We should have been issued B-4 bags by now, but I think they are waiting until we don't need them so much. If you ever wonder why I find the army dull, go stand on the sidewalk in the sun for an hour before each meal with a gathering of neighbors around you moaning and complaining.

                                                                     Love, Roger

November 15, 1944
Tampa, Fla.
Dear Mother:

    Four hundred boys live in my room, the chow isn't fit for low-grade hogs, and we are going through basic training again. I was recently placed on garbage collecting for some slight shortcoming. Still, I am prepared to like it here. If I am flying, I get my chute and Mae West checked out, wait for the officers to be briefed, and load into a truck to be taken out to the B-17. The field is a huge network of cement and when we start down the runway I am plenty confused, but we usually hit the right one. When we take off, I love to hear the motors roar and be pressed back against my "arm chair."

The pilot is a nice young thing from Ohio who seems to know a lot about his business in the air. The co-pilot is the prize of the crew, a jolly, lecherous fellow, older than the rest and with good mechanical sense. The bombardier seems to be typical of his gang, drops his bombs at the right times and then sleeps off his hangovers. The radio gunner (me) is, of course, terrific.

Do you know anyone in Tampa, another Smithie, for instance?

Love, Roger

Jan. 24, 1945
Savannah, Ga.
Dear Dad:

We left MacDill [AFB] last Friday for an all-night train trip to this so-called "staging area" and have been processing and getting quantities of new amazing equipment. I am back in my old habit of sleeping till noon which is beneficial for my outlook. I have been afraid that I would never be able to acquire that habit again, and it has taken a week of diligent practice to achieve it. Now we sit and wait.

Love, Roger

March 22, 1945
England
Dear Dad:

Marvelous trip over, quite an experience for a gang flown in circles for months. We stayed in Iceland for a while. Weather Unbelievably foul! Quarters? Poor, and not improved by the crew who shared our hole and played cards all night. Wales was a welcome sight with so much green after the bleakness of Iceland. We were assigned to a comfortable hut and were welcomed by a genial crew who were celebrating the completion of their mission. Celebrations being my thing, I helped.

Love, Roger

April 5, 1945
England
Dear Dad:

A few visits to the Reich are behind me and before long we will be veterans at this game, having flown for ten straight days. We are awakened about 2 a.m. for breakfast and briefing, check the ship and wait for take-off which may be hours later. After the mission, we are issued a most welcome double shot of cognac, reverse the process and make it to bed before the man comes around again. (I love to pull in the news stations on our way home. How about getting a good set for the living room?)

Love, Roger

April 13, 1945
England
Dear Mother:

It is hard to imagine our country without F.D.R., but we'd better get used to it in order to continue his work at a crucial time. I've done a fair amount of sightseeing—Buckingham Palace, Westminster, Scotland Yard, etc. and got a good glimpse of the bawdy night life here. We also went to a dance hall where a good supply of "finch" was on hand. The "Limey" girls dress poorly, jitterbug madly, and are very jolly as a rule.

Love, Roger

May 8, 1945
England
Dear Mother:

Much good cheer on the island! Peace at last to the starving, battered countries of Europe and to the families at home who are sweating out sons in the front lines; this is why the suffering has been endured. We have flown over cities from low altitude, and the devastation is beyond belief. The boys with a lot of missions will go home soon, and we will get some concentrated training for who knows what.

Love, Roger

June 21, 1945
Bury St. Edmunds, England
Dear Mother:

 In answer to your questions, we have credit for 12 missions; two to Kiel where the flak was heavy and we got presidential citations, one to Parchein in northern Germany, Planen, Neurenberg, Brandenberg, Denmark, and Munich. Rumor has it that we will be going over soon, perhaps near Lake Constance where we will be in a Troop Carrier Squadron ferrying troops and equipment.

Love, Roger

July 28, 1945
Bury St. Edmunds, England
Dear Grandmother:

 We just completed a concentrated ferry job, carrying the last of the 55th Fighter Group to their new field near Munich. The field is formerly a Luftwaffe cadet base and is one of the few that was not bombed on the whole continent. Our future field, on the other hand, has been bombed to bits including the runways and every last building. I think we will have to live in the next town. Today we buzzed the Eiffel Tower in a demonstration. We came in plenty low with a fighter escort and gave a good show.

Love, Roger

August 28, 1945
Bury St. Edmunds, England
Dear Father:

 VJ Day and peace are so important as no more friends will be killed and relief will come to the world. It will be a long time until gas rationing is over here, and the food situation is not improving, an uphill fight for this crowd. I had a five-day pass, and everywhere I went the "quiet, reserved" Limeys were whooping it up. I was trying to get some Canadian gal home, and at each side street the local crowd dragged us in for some brew and dancing. We took the "long way home." I have put in 50-100 flight hours a month since VE Day. Yesterday I had breakfast in Africa, dinner in Germany, and bedtime in England. Strange, isn't it?

Love, Staff Sgt. Roger

October 24, 1945
Wiesbaden, Germany
Dear Mother:

The situation doesn't look nearly as bleak as it did at first, largely due to the fact that a G.I. expects little and can settle down in anything from a castle to a foxhole. Latrines and sidewalks are being built, and perhaps this windswept mud-hole will look like an air base before long. We make regularly scheduled runs to Berlin, Paris, Munich, Bremen and London. As the radio operator, I am the only enlisted man in the crew and must act as engineer, crew chief, stewardess, and general slave when not working the radio! Ike has sent out a directive about the advantages of a winter sports program for the troops, and I looked into it. I was on orders to go to a ski school in the Alps, but some Major got wind of it and stopped it. I may wangle it later.

Love, Roger

November 11, 1945
Wiesbaden, Germany
Dear Mother:

It is my birthday, and, to put it rather mildly, it is a privilege to be able to write today. Yesterday I was fortunate enough to walk away from a flaming C-47 after a crash landing on a mountainside near Koblenz in French-occupied Germany with nothing but a few cuts and bruises to show for it. I thought for a while that I was going to die there because I was too short to reach the escape hatch, but another crew mate was behind me and gave me a boost. We ran down the wing, and I think I was still running in the air! It is in the miracle class when five crew members and twenty-two passengers can get through to tell about it. The loss of some good clothes, a pair of Aunt Rose's hand-knit socks, and my Thayer-McNeal shoes annoys me, although I suppose that was a pretty good bargain.

Could you send me a pair of garters and a toilet article kit?

Love, Roger

January 13, 1946
Nice, France
Dear Dad:

I think this is the most desirable place in the ETO with

tennis, skiing, dancing, beautiful girls, warm sunshine, good food, great hotel and all that make Nice and the Rivera famous. On the way here, our pilot, (I called him "Billy, the boy pilot") tried to land our C-47 like he did his former B-17s, over-did it, bounced down the runway as few planes have ever bounced, sheered several inches off the props and ended up in the Mediterranean. The fans on the sidelines gave us one chance in ten to make it through alive, and we did! The boys now call me "Lucky" as I only had minor cuts to show for the adventure. Never fret, old boy, this was my last trip.

Love, Roger

P.S. A double engine change will be necessary, and there are no engines here, so I think I will go skiing.

January 29, 1946
Furstenfeldbruck, Germany
Dear Mother:

I have finished processing at a casual redeployment center and am waiting at the pipeline entrance for the starter's gun. I'd like to beat this letter home.

Love, Roger

Born and raised in the Boston area, Roger summered in Grafton, Vt. He attended the Putney School and graduated from Harvard College in 1943. He worked as a consultant in employee benefits. An avid skier who supported and enjoyed ski racing for more than 75 years, he had six children and four step-children.

The War in Photos

A view of the invasion of Normandy on D-Day, June 6, 1944. Provided by Phil Stoddard who fought with the Third Armored Division across France and into Germany. See story, Page 81.

Kes Schoepf started his training with the Royal Canadian Air Force before transferring back to the Army Air Corps in 1941. He was killed over Salerno, Italy in August 1943. His sister Julie Crocker's story is found on Page 188.

Famed movie actress Marlene Dietrich borrows the violin of Army orchestra member Nathan Gottschalk (front left) during a rehearsal for Irving Berlin's musical This is the Army. *Her bow and fingering positions were perfect because, as she told the orchestra members, she got her start in show business playing the violin and singing in nightclubs. At that night's performance, she appeared on stage in a slinky, high-slit dress to the roaring approval of the troops. Nathan's wife Polly's story is found on Page 199.*

Roger B. Wilson on sentry duty at an Army encampment. His war experiences are related in a series of letters home, beginning on Page 99.

Peter Oliver's story of the war years in Lebanon, Egypt and Iraq is found on Page 73. Tanks and armored vehicles played a large role in battles in the Middle East.

Before the British invaded Iraq, the Nazis maintained air bases there. From the story by Peter Oliver, Page 73.

Above, units of the Third Armored Division take a breather during the push across Europe. (Phil Stoddard, Page 81.)
Below, not every landing was picture perfect in the combat environment. (Roger Wilson, Page 99).

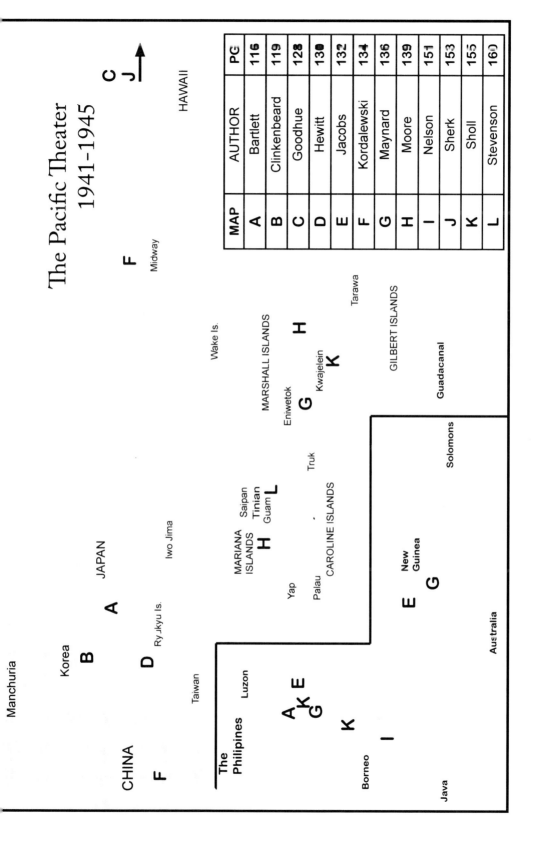

PART TWO

The Pacific Theater
THE 70-TON CRANE THAT SENT US HOME

SHEPPARD BARTLETT

I was Stores Officer on the *LST 593*, one of many LSTs which carried men and supplies all over the world. They were the workhorses of invasions and landings, and so it was for *LST 593*. For almost a year we sailed around the Philippines and other Pacific Islands shifting troops and equipment, and we participated in three invasions.

In time we were informed that we would be converted into a Hospital ship and an attack missile launcher! We had vast space below deck for medical sick bays and operations, and compartments with bunks for eight or ten men. A doctor who was a full commander was assigned to our ship with medical personnel, and started setting up their operation. As Stores Officer, I had to make plans for food service and order supplies. Our main deck was going to be outfitted with missile platforms for firing missiles as we beached. It was an exciting time.

And then came the bombs, atomic bombs! The world changed overnight. August 6th and 9th, 1945, the U.S. attacked and bombed two cities in Japan and by August 15 Japan surrendered. The whole Japanese attack plan was canceled; the doctor left our ship and went home!

We were on our way to San Pedro Bay and the Navy Base at Guivan, scheduled for a hull scrape-down on September 1st. It took us four days and we had orders to prepare for a trip to Japan.

We spent the next two weeks readying the ship: fuel, food for 200 men, and we started picking up CBs, the construction and building division of the Navy, heavy equipment, rolling stock, trucks and dozers. We filled our tank deck and main deck topside, and at the last minute, a 70-ton crane was rolled onto our tank deck just behind the big bow doors. Nothing could come off our ship until that crane was removed.

On September 20th we were in convoy with 40 LSTs, a few freighters and 3 destroyer escorts on the first flotilla to go to Japan. The LSTs were loaded with CBs and heavy equipment but we were the only ship with a 70-ton crane! On September 29th we arrived in Tokyo Bay and anchored. We were 200 feet from the U.S.S. *Missouri*, the ship where the Japanese had officially surrendered to General McArthur.

After two days it was discovered that there was no suitable area where we could unload the 70-ton crane. This meant that nothing could be unloaded from our ship. So we upped anchor and headed north to Shiogama in the Sendai area of Honshu. On October 3 we anchored in the outer harbor in deep water. It took 90 fathoms of chain to hold us. Tornado warnings sent us to the inner harbor through salt marshes loaded with oyster-farm frames. Two days later we were informed that there was no area here where we could unload a 70-ton crane! So we set sail for the west coast of Honshu, sailing up north through the Honshu Straits and south along the coast to the Senami area. We would be met on a beach there. While we were going through the Honshu Straits, the 70-ton crane broke loose, and it took breath-taking efforts to re-shackle it. On October 16th we arrived at the beach area and proceeded to hit the beach. The weather was stormy with big waves, and we hit the beach with a bang...a big bang, enough bang that it bent the nose of the ship up into the bow doors! The doors would not open. The weight of the crane contributed to the crunch. Fortunately the CBs on the beach had two bulldozers, and by using them with a little TNT, they were able to force the bow doors open. We were finally able to move that 70-ton crane off the ship so we could unload the rest of our men and equipment. To close the bow doors so we could leave, we had to call the two bulldozers into play again, literally dozing the doors together so they could be shackled, but the nose of the ship was still badly damaged.

On October 21 we arrived back in Yokohama Bay to get our orders and prepare for the trip back to the Philippines. We did get to go ashore in all the areas we visited. We found the country had footpaths and fast trains between cities, but few roads. The autos and trucks we saw were operating on charcoal since there was no gasoline. The people we met were so happy the war was over. They were friendly to us, invited us to their public baths and showed us their gardens. There was little that we could buy in the way of gifts and we were told not to eat their food.

We saw weapons of all kinds piled two stories high behind the town halls. General MacArthur had sternly ordered that anyone found with any type of arms would be shot. It worked, no one was shot. The country was obviously devastated, but we detected a sense of "let's get on with it and create a new country." The past is over! On the 24th we said good-bye to Japan and left with a small convoy.

We arrived back at Subic Bay in the Philippines on Nov. 1st and went into dry-dock for inspection of our damaged bow, and we were placed on limited service. On Nov 20th we were ordered home, back to the States. Fueled up and loaded with food, we were on our way on the 21st. It took us only 17 days, 20 hours to reach Pearl Harbor. We had 210 men, 12 officers when we arrived. We reached San Diego on Dec 20th, then continued on through the Panama Canal and home to Charleston, S.C. in late February. The ship was decommissioned in mid March. I was the only officer that stayed on the ship from commissioning date to decommissioning date. It was quite an adventure.

Shep was born in Lowell, Mass., and attended Mount Hermon School. After the war, he completed his degree at Syracuse University and spent his career in advertising design and retailing. A member of the Rotary Club for more than 60 years, Shep has spent the last 16 years of retirement as a S.C.O.R.E. counselor in southern New Hampshire. He and his wife Amy have three children.

From the Coast Guard to Korea

David Clinkenbeard

In 1944, the year I graduated from high school, the choices with respect to military service were simple. Upon reaching age 18 you were obligated to register for the draft. Alternatively, at age 17 or before being conscripted, one could enlist in any of the military services. For me the choice was simple, being somewhat of sound mind and in good health, military service was inevitable. Since I was not yet 18, I could wait the better part of a year and expect to be drafted, or I could enlist. Waiting was a poor choice as the risk of starting college was that one might not finish the term. Seeking employment was pretty much of a non-starter as firms were less than anxious to hire anyone subject to near-term departure for the service, at least with respect to attractive jobs.

For me the choice of which service to enter was not difficult. Living three houses away on our block in Seattle was a fine gentleman who had retired prior to Pearl Harbor as a chief warrant officer in the Coast Guard with 30 years of service. When the war started in December 1941, the Coast Guard prevailed on my neighbor to re-enter active duty and they made him a commissioned officer and appointed him as the Recruiting Officer for the 13th Coast Guard District Headquarters in Seattle. My mother made the choice for me by remarking that she would be unable to face our neighbors if I went anywhere but in the Coast Guard. It was a done deal.

What might appear as a windfall was that apparently a lot of other young men also wanted to serve in the Coast Guard, and as a result, the boot camps were full and one had to wait their turn to serve. In the fullness of time, a train load of us set off from Seattle to Alameda, Calif., for eight weeks of introduction to military service. Most of the graduates of our class went off to sea, but for reasons that were minimally apparent to me, I was selected to attend the Navy's Aerographers Mate School at the Naval Air Station, Lakehurst, N.J. The base was also the location of the Navy's lighter-than-air dirigibles and their parachute training facility.

Aerographers were what was known in Navy terminology as "wind sniffers." The training, which was all by young commissioned officers, many of whom had university degrees in meteorology, was to prepare graduates to draw weather maps and make forecasts. Most graduates were assigned to air stations.

Duty at N.A.S. Lakehurst was somewhat less than arduous. While the classes were intense, weekends were mostly free and it was easy to hitchhike to Atlantic City, Philadelphia or New York. It certainly was a far cry from being in a foxhole and that made me appreciate my mother's good judgment in sending me to the Coast Guard.

My good luck certainly held out as I was one of three in the class who did well enough to be awarded the rank of Aerographers Mate Third Class upon graduation. The stripe was a wonderful reward for a kid who had just turned 18 years of age. The better reward was that I was given a choice of assignments, most of which were at Coast Guard air stations in the continental United States. At that age, I was less adventurous than I now wish I had been, so I chose the closest facility to my Seattle home, which was the U.S. Coast Guard Air Station, South San Francisco, Calif., which, in fact, turned out to be the San Francisco airport. The Coast Guard had space at the north end of the field where the Pan American Airline clippers had berthed.

Our mission was air-sea rescue with a mix of amphibious aircraft including PBYs, PBMs, PB2Y4s and some other monsters that the Navy had pawned off on the Coast Guard. There were three of us assigned to weather forecasting and the job primarily involved getting up early in the morning and drawing a weather map based on radio transmission of weather data - temperature, barometric pressure, dew point, cloud structure (type, height, coverage), wind direction and intensity, precipitation and some other factors that now escape my memory. Since this was a continual exercise — every day of the year and more frequently if needed — we "wind sniffers" could follow weather patterns and chart the movement of frontal conditions. In fact, given the peculiar weather conditions in San Francisco, a major element of the task was forecasting when the fog would lift to permit visual flight rules performance.

It would be hard to imagine a more enjoyable assignment than what I had at USCG Air Station, South San Francisco. The war in Europe had ended and the U.S. and allied position in the Pacific was increasingly dominant. Most nights were free and downtown San Francisco was a $1 bus trip away. I was in the city the night the Japanese surrender was announced. Our discharge from service came only a few weeks later. A grateful nation was kind enough to give me the G.I. Bill and other benefits for 14 months of duty that was so trivial in comparison with what others experienced. I am thankful for the experience and being able to serve. My only wish is that I could have made a more important contribution to my country in that historic period.

Korea

Along with millions of other GIs, I entered university in the fall of 1946. For many of us, the G.I. Bill was a windfall and made a college education an obvious choice. However, the stipend did not cover all of the costs so I looked for another option. At the time, many colleges and universities had ROTC programs that recruited both veterans and those who had not served. While the monetary compensation was not substantial it was a nice supplement to what the G.I. Bill provided.

The added advantage for veterans was that you entered the Advanced Program in the Army ROTC and received your commission as a Second Lieutenant in two years. It was too good a deal to pass up. Most nonveterans in the ROTC had a four-year program and after being commissioned spent two years on active duty. Those of us who were veterans were assigned to the Reserves and were only called to active duty when the Korean War resulted in a shortfall of company grade officers.

Those of us who were called to active duty were informed that our service would be for two years unless we elected to serve longer. Soon after being activated, I applied for and was accepted to train as an Army Aviator as I had a long interest in flying and was impressed by the advantage of having the service underwrite the cost of my learning to fly. At the time I entered the program, they were designated as Liaison Pilots and the wings we wore had a capital "L" in the center.

Our flight training was provided by the Air Force at Waco Air Force Base, (now the Connally AFB) in Waco, Tex. Our class of 32 officers, ranging in rank from Major to Second Lieutenant, was the first in a number of years as it was only with the outbreak of the Korean War that the Army had need for additional aviators. We flew the L-16 which was essentially the Aeronica widely used by civilian flyers equipped with an 85 horsepower Lycoming engine. After the customary eight hours of flight instruction, I soloed and finished the program to get my Liaison Pilot wings. All of those graduating were transferred to Fort Sill in Lawton, Okla., where the Artillery School was located along with the the Army Aviation School. The thirteen-week program concentrated on short field landings and takeoffs — a lot of low and slow flying. Fort Sill abuts the Wichita Mountain National Wildlife Refuge where the Army maintained a maze of cleared air strips abundantly populated by rattlesnakes and other miscreant creatures, at least in the summertime. A popular exercise was to spot a snake lying in the sun in the landing area and try to touch down directly on top of the reptile. Another popular summertime diversion was to land next to a watermelon field and quickly swipe a sample.

About the time of our graduation in December 1950, the Army had done away with the Liaison Pilot designation and we were awarded the aeronautical designation of "ARMY AVIATOR BY ORDER OF THE SECRETARY OF THE ARMY." Hot stuff!

For reasons known only to some factotum somewhere in the Army, two other graduates and I were asked to stay on at Fort Sill and become Flight Instructors. In my case, at least, it wasn't because I had distinguished myself in the course or demonstrated superior flying skills. In the military, one learns to just go with the flow and not question the logic behind decisions in which you have no involvement. So for the next ten months I was a flight instructor with a common routine of sitting in the back seat of a small plane being flown by a student who I knew was trying to kill us both. It became obvious that the need for additional pilots resulted in a less rigorous practice of "washing out" students who had marginal skills. My personal concern was passing a student who was not fully qualified and who might go on to have an accident because of that failing. During this period at Fort Sill, I also completed the helicopter pilot training in the Bell Ranger H-13.

In early October 1951 when my obligatory two-year tour of duty was about to expire, I was notified that since Army Aviators were in short supply, those of us with that military occupation specialty (MOS) would be involuntarily extended with no definite date for discharge indicated. We were also offered the option of voluntarily extending with the assurance that we would remain at Fort Sill as instructors in the Army Aviation Tactical School. The choice wasn't difficult for me as I wanted to get out as soon as possible and attend law school. Once I declined the Army's generous offer, the orders to Korea came almost instantly. In early November, I was on a charter flight from Seattle to Tokyo and then on to Inchon and to my first assignment.

I filled a temporary billet as a helicopter pilot with the First Mobile Army Surgical Hospital in the northeast corner of South Korea. The time was at the end of the major battles known as "Heartbreak Ridge" and "The Punch Bowl." It is difficult to adequately describe the extraordinary contribution that the MASH units made to our effort in Korea. At our unit, except for the regular army commanding officer, a Medical Corps lieutenant colonel and his executive officer, a major, all the medical officers were young doctors—most of them just out of their internship. Many medical students at that time obtained a deferment from military service but were called up quickly after finishing their studies. Many of them were sent to Korea soon thereafter. What they may have lacked in experience they more than made up for in enthusiasm and commitment. The challenge of doing medical procedures, particularly surgery, that they might not have encountered in a civilian medical practice for many years or not at all, was a strong motivator. We three pilots and our ground crew were motivated as well by their example.

Our routine as pilots was rather uncomplicated. Urgent calls came in by radio telephone to pick up one or more wounded soldiers within our geographical area (X Corps). The Bell Ranger H-13 was equipped with an outboard stretcher on each side and a seat next to the pilot which mobile evacuees could use. The helicopters in the early 1950s lacked the more powerful engines that are common today and the helicopter was essentially an unstable aircraft. It could not be flown "hands off." Further, it was unstable in a way that fixed wing aircraft were not. While one could land a helicopter that had engine failure, if any structural part failed, after being hit by ground fire for example, the machine could fall to the ground. While parachutes were always part of the equipment for fixed-wing military aircraft, they were useless in rotary aircraft. Our ability to respond was also limited by the fact that we could safely transport only two, and on rare occasions three, casualties in an aircraft designed for only two persons. That's why we never carried a corpsman with us to attend to the wounded. One of our pilots often met the challenge to carry back a full load. I never had the confidence in my flying skills to try it.

The Medical Services Corps officer in charge of admissions and logistics would respond to the call from the field and the bell would ring for us. We rotated assignments and would receive the map coordinates or designated landing area and number of casualties from the incoming message. With an excellent ground crew we could be airborne in minutes. Time was always of the essence and a life might be saved by fast response. The medical personnel were alerted by our flight departure and were prepared to receive the soldiers instantly on our return touchdown. It was not exceptional to have a soldier undergoing surgery within an hour of the time he became a casualty. Therein lies the overwhelming contribution that this system provided for the first time in our military experience.

For me, this was a high-stress experience. First, I hadn't enough helicopter pilot hours to make me comfortable with my abilities. Second, it was difficult flying. The terrain and weather in our area were always challenging. Lastly, we were constantly aware that a badly injured soldier's life might be saved if we got him to the hospital in time.

There were compensations, however. Life with the medics was a lot better than what most experienced in the combat area. I'm sure the food was better, the company of highly intelligent and spirited doctors was delightful and there were even nurses about, which struck me as not part of the milieu of hazardous duty. There was even a sort of Officers' Club where cocktails were available before the evening meal. Officers got a monthly ration of one fifth of spirits, usually scotch whiskey that was probably distilled in Japan. The doctors, however, collectively had scientific skills which allowed them to manufacture their own distillates. None died of thirst.

I was not unhappy when at the latter part of my second month I was reassigned to do what I had come to Korea expecting to do. I was assigned as Air Officer of the 96th Field Artillery Battalion, a 155mm howitzer unit with all white officers and all black enlisted men. How times have changed. This assignment was what I had been trained to do, and I was confident that I could perform competently. Each artillery battalion had two aircraft and two pilots with a ground crew of three mechanics.

We flew the L-19, a plane made by Cessna and particularly designed for the task of short field landings and takeoffs. While at Fort Sill, I had taken delivery at the Cessna factory in Wichita, Kansas of the fifth L-19 procured by the Army. The L-19 was an excellent plane and could do whatever we asked of it. Our field was 900 feet in length - not all of it useable. This created an interesting challenge in cross wind landings and takeoffs. The battalion had two artillery observers who usually, but not always, flew with us, sitting in the back seat and looking for enemy targets appropriate for calling in our howitzers.

We frequently flew solo and did the artillery adjustment ourselves. Obviously, most of our time was spent flying over enemy lines as that was where we could find the targets. The hazard lay in that we also flew at low altitudes, the better to find targets. A great find would be a tank; but trucks, other vehicles and troop emplacements were more common targets. The mountainous terrain gave the North Koreans the opportunity to park their men and equipment on the back side of the hills where artillery was difficult to reach them.

Nevertheless, there were enough moving targets to make our effort worthwhile. Most days each of us battalion pilots flew one mission of 3 to 4 hours, the limitation being the fuel capacity of the L-19 and the need to stay within range of our landing strip. Unfortunately for me, my flying colleague had a proclivity for sick days so that I often flew his scheduled mission as well as my own.

Flying seven or eight hours north of the front line made for a very long day. The only precaution that one could take was to keep moving and gain altitude whenever it appeared to be the prudent course. Fortunately, the North Koreans did not have aircraft to protect their front lines, but ground fire was a constant threat. It was reported that Army aviators had the highest mortality rate among officers in Korea, although I am not sure of the accuracy of that report. I did lose friends, including a pilot who had been one of my Fort Sill students. That is what happens in war.

Our planes had no armor protection. My mechanic, however, found a flak jacket which he reworked into a cushion that I would sit on while flying. I can't say that it saved my life, or anything else, but it was comforting to have it. The few of us who were hit by ground fire mostly survived because a critical part of the plane was not hit, but it certainly put us on notice to head home or somewhere else.

During the 1951-52 period while I was in Korea, the intensity of the combat, at least in the X Corps area, tapered off. In fact, in my last several months, I believe it is accurate to say that the U.S. forces lost more men to vehicular accidents and to epidemic hemorrhagic fever than to enemy action. However, there were periods when action flared up, so the tension remained.

One morning in early May, 1952 the Battalion Adjutant sent a jeep to the airstrip with a message that he urgently needed to see me. I had a mission to fly so our meeting was put off until the afternoon. The subject of the meeting was an order received from the Department of the Army stating that all officers involuntarily extended had to be sent home for discharge and that he had only three days to get me on my way to Sasebo in Japan for shipment home. Apparently, I was the only officer in the battalion in this category and was specifically named in the order, so I got all of his attention. I had little difficulty in complying with his request to get moving.

Getting home was an adventure, the most interesting part being that everyone went home by sea. The reason, it was rumored, was so we could be wormed in transit, given the prevalence of parasites in Korea. I ended up at Fort Lawton, Wash., free of worms, with a transfer to the Reserves, a Bronze Star and an Air Medal with two Oak Leaf Clusters, and 104 missions to my credit.

Memories after 60 years are peculiar. I barely remember the hardship that combat conditions imposed. I do recall the pleasant incidents that did occur. Most specifically, one event still gives me pleasure. I befriended a master sergeant in Corps headquarters by flying him somewhere he wanted to go. He reciprocated by inviting me to headquarters to take home with me whatever quantity of ice cream from the Commanding General's mess I could get in the back of the L-19. Ice cream was, as far as I knew, not available anywhere else in the combat zone. Our small contingent at the airfield — 2 pilots, 3 mechanics and a Korean houseboy - couldn't make a dent in what I brought back so I ferried it to the MASH. The highlight was with the Korean houseboy (age 16 or 17) who had the first taste in his life of ice cream. It was such a delight for all of us that it is imprinted in my mind.

My military career covered 5 years and 4 months of active duty. While I would have preferred to have spent that time doing other things, I remember mostly the good times that I had in the service. The Korean tour of duty was probably the only penance that I had to pay for the cushy time I had in the Coast Guard during World War II. In the end, it is not only a duty but an honor to serve our country in whatever way it asks us to serve. I am proud to have served.

Born in Seattle, Wash., David graduated from the University of Washington and earned his J.D. at Harvard Law School. He worked in management consulting for Arthur D. Little, Inc. and was a vice president at American Express Co. He was a director of Athens College and a trustee of Vermont Academy. He and his wife Barbara have two children and two grandchildren.

The Irony of War

John Goodhue

Japan attacked Pearl Harbor in December of 1941. The next day President Roosevelt declared war on Japan. I was sixteen and still in school. The war tightened our school routine. We had war service classes for map reading, in which I did well, and radio, in which I did badly. We mounted the tower of our chapel to spot airplanes which we seriously believed could be hostile.

That summer found me at Castle Island in South Boston working on the construction of a massive new cargo terminal. There the Army could store and load out their supplies for troops stationed all around the world. It was the first time that I worked on the Fourth of July instead of setting off fire crackers and rockets. Perhaps that was a more meaningful Fourth.

In January of 1943 I turned eighteen and enlisted in a Marine Corps training program that would let me complete my education. The Army had similar programs that enlisted some of my friends. We were all eager to get involved.

After completing my educational requirements, I found myself at the Marine Corps Recruit Depot on Parris Island, S. C. My personality was reduced to zero. Two Marine corporals and a platoon sergeant awaited my arrival. They were dedicated to the creed that no Marine ghost would ever return to haunt them with the fact that training failure had cost him his life. We were shepherded through our paces — running. We learned that bayonets were used for cleaning cracks in barracks floors as well as for killing the enemy. We marched, we drilled, we cleaned and we learned to respond instantly, unquestioningly, to all orders.

One of our recruits, Ben, received a letter from his girl. It was addressed to Bennie. "Have we ever heard of a Marine called Bennie?" That was the question. The label belabored our friend throughout his training.

We fired our rifles; not our guns. We won honors, if we lived up to the high standards for Marine marksmanship. Laggards were harassed unmercifully. Many dropped out.

We were all transformed into something new called a *Marine*. On leaving Parris Island, training persisted in the swamps and jungles of North Carolina and Virginia, known only to the Marine Corps.

My Marine training program continued, even as the Pacific War progressed inexorably towards its ultimate goal, the Japanese homeland. In the meantime my friends in the Army were called out of their programs, with minimal training, to stem the massive, violent German drive in December of 1944. They saw major action. Many were lost, before the European War terminated in May.

In April the Okinawa Campaign came and went successfully. My training intensified in anticipation of the Japanese homeland invasion. Then in August of 1945 the atomic bomb was dropped and the war ended.

All that training. All that planning. All those Marines. No Japanese invasion. Demobilization. It was all over.

A native of Boston, Mass., John grew up in the Long Island community of Hewlett, N.Y. He attended Milton Academy and Harvard College and spent his career in the ocean transportation industry. He and his wife Charlotte have five children.

THE COMBAT PIANO PLAYER

PETER HEWITT

Most of us still laugh about the ridiculous things that happened while we were in uniform. In most cases we've been able to sweep the grim stuff under the rug.

For me, my entire "military" experience was pretty ridiculous. Robert Benchley could have written one of his delightful stories about it.

It started out typically screwed up. I had enlisted in the Army Air Force, hoping to become a flyer. After basic training (where I actually gained weight), they closed the program down, there then being an oversupply of guys with wings. I was then trained to be an airplane mechanic. Just as the war ended I shipped out to Okinawa to serve as a mechanic with the 8th Air Force which had by then relocated from England.

After a couple of weeks living in a tent awaiting assignment, I was called on by Warrant Officer Irving Lilly and First Sergeant Jack Snodgrass (real names) of the 558th Army Air Force band. Mister Lilly, the bandleader (warrant officers were addressed as "mister"), invited (not ordered) me to join the band, explaining that they wanted a piano player to replace the present piano man who was about to go home "on points," having been in the Pacific area a couple of years.

After about 30 seconds of deliberation I replied in the affirmative. (When the band marched, I would play bass drum, cymbals or glockenspiel.) When I asked what they had for a piano, it turned out to be an indestructible little Steinway made especially for the army!

Mister Lilly was a piece of work. In real life he taught kids how to play the violin, but as an army bandleader he had delusions of grandeur. He requisitioned a command car (there were still a few around) and drove it around Okinawa as if he had four stars on his shoulders.

One of our trumpet players was a great jazz man. When we were scheduled to play for a review for a visiting general, he suggested that we bag the usual Sousa march and play the Tiger Rag instead. It really swung and we got a letter of commendation.

The nearest thing to a war story that I can come up with has to do with our little dance band (the "Esquires"). We were to play for a detachment of troops on Ie Shima, a small island off the coast of Okinawa. We were flown over in a tired-looking B-25. The little Steinway didn't fit, but there was a wreck of a piano on Ie Shima that was so flat I had to transpose everything we played to be in tune with the rest of the band.

The following day we piled back into our old B-25. As we were about to take off, the pilot shut down the engines and ordered us all off the plane. He then started the engines and charged down the runway. He piled up on a mini-mountain of coral. It turned out there were no brakes.

So ends the account of my heroic war career.

A native of Cambridge, Mass., Peter graduated from Harvard College and spent his career in the manufacturing and banking industries. He has three children.

From Convoys to Weather

Carl B. Jacobs

When I heard the news of the Pearl Harbor attack on December 7, 1941, I was having dinner with friends in Chicago. At the time, I was working for Inland Steel which I joined shortly after graduating from Princeton in 1941.

My undergraduate program was science and mathematics and I had intended to go for additional work in engineering. With the military draft in force, I decided to sign up with the U. S. Navy. I was called to duty on December 8, 1941, and reported to the U. S Navy training ship *Prairie State* in New York harbor for a four-month officer training course.

Upon graduating, I was selected to continue for nine month's duty as a part of the staff on the *Prairie State* and on May 12, 1942, I graduated with a commission, got married and reported for duty at my new station. Ann and I were fortunate to find an apartment in New York City and there were several other officers and families in the same building.

When the duty on the *Prairie State* ended, I asked to be sent to diesel engine school at Ithaca, N.Y. This was to be my engineering billet on board, as many of the new Navy ships being built at the time were diesel powered. I studied the Detroit Winton diesel engines and in late 1943 was sent to Miami for ship assignment.

The ship on which I was to be the Engineering Officer was the U.S.S. *PCE 875*. This was a 185-foot ship designed to escort convoys. While most of the crew remained in San Pedro, Calif., for training, the Captain, the Supply Officer and I went to Portland, Ore., where the ship was being built, to help with the fitting out. The ship was commissioned on January 19, 1944 and, after sea trials, was sent through the Panama Canal to Trinidad to be used for convoy escort to Brazil. I made several convoy trips with her until December 1944, when the ship was sent to Key West, Fla., for overhaul.

In January 1945, the ship, on which I was now the Executive Officer, was sent to the Pacific for duty. The convoys that the ship escorted went from New Guinea to Leyte Gulf in the Philippines to provide supplies for the invasion of Luzon.

In December 1944, Typhoon Cobra inflicted severe damage on Navy ships in the area about 300 miles east of Leyte. Among the reasons for the severity of the damage was that inadequate weather information had been available to the Pacific Fleet in that area. As a result, some ships were converted in early 1945 to weather duty and the *PCE 875* was one of them. We cruised in an area between Guam and Leyte to report the weather until V-J Day, August 15, 1945.

With the war over, I returned to Chicago to take up duties at Inland Steel, from which I retired in 1980.

A native of Bethlehem, Pa., Carl spent most of his adult life in Glenview, Ill. He is a graduate of the Phillips Academy, Andover and Princeton University and spent his career with the Inland Steel Co., retiring as vice president, raw materials in 1980. He and his wife Ann had three children.

THE RIGHT PLACE AT THE RIGHT TIME

ANDREW KORDALEWSKI

Being in the right place at the right time is kind of the story of my life. After high school, I went to a radio school in Boston to get some practical experience. This then lead me to a job at a radio station in Laconia, N.H. During lunch hours at the local drug store, I made friends with a Marine Corps recruiting sergeant who helped me decide to enlist in the Marine Corps rather than get drafted.

So that's what I did on December 8, 1942, one year and a day after Pearl Harbor. By enlisting, I was able to continue my work in radio and was sent to electronics school at the Naval Research Laboratory in Washington after completing my basic training at Camp Lejeune in North Carolina.

When the time came to ship out, I was sent to Midway Island in the Pacific as a sergeant in a defense battalion responsible for maintaining the island's communications and electronic equipment. Fortunately this was after the Battle of Midway. This battle was the most important naval battle of the war in the Pacific. It occurred between July 4 - 7, 1942 when the United States Navy defeated a Japanese naval attack against Midway Atoll causing incredible damage to the Japanese fleet.

I remained at Midway for about a year and then was shipped to Hawaii where I joined the 1st Marine Division in preparation for the invasion of Japan. Fortunately Japan surrendered before we were activated. Since I didn't have enough points for discharge, I was sent to Tin Sin, China to operate an Armed Forces radio station until I was finally discharged toward the end of 1945. I was just 22 years old and was grateful to have my whole life ahead of me.

So I went back to school on the GI Bill for more electronics and then to Gettysburg College where I majored in physics. I graduated in 1952 just in time to ride the wave of the transistor era. My wife and I settled in Syracuse, N.Y., where I was fortunate to remain through technical careers with General Electric, Carrier Corporation and Niagara Mohawk.

The best thing for me was that first job at the radio station in Laconia. It pointed me in a direction that I was able to follow for the rest of my life. I guess I was in the right place at the right time.

Born in Johnston, R.I., Andrew grew up on a chicken farm in Hinsdale, Mass. After his service in the war, he majored in physics at Gettysburg College and later earned a graduate degree from Syracuse University. Andrew spent his career in the electronics industry. He often volunteered for the Red Cross. He and his wife Jean had one son.

Destroyer Duty in the North Atlantic and South Pacific

Doug Maynard

It is true that in joining the Navy I didn't see the world but I did see more than enough of the North Atlantic and the South Pacific.

After graduating from college in the spring of 1941, I entered the Navy as a midshipman in September. We were the "ninety-day wonders" who were to be converted from recent college graduates into Navy ensigns in three months' time. The attack on Pearl Harbor on December 7 speeded up the process and I soon found myself on a destroyer in the North Atlantic about to receive authentic on-the-job training.

The role of the Navy at that time was to make it possible to transfer enormous quantities of supplies and large numbers of men and their weapons from North America to Europe. Destroyers were given the task of searching for enemy submarines and shepherding convoys of merchant ships and warships across the Atlantic.

In the North Atlantic, weather conditions, especially in midwinter, could be almost as challenging as German submarines. Destroyers, the smallest ships of the fleet, were designed for speed and maneuverability, not seaworthiness or stability. When a storm intensifies it becomes more and more difficult to both contend with the storm and still keep position in the convoy or in the screen. There were times when the convoy commodore had to break up the formation and pass the signal for each ship to save itself and rendezvous two or three days later at some point "X" further along the track.

Toward the end of 1942 the routine of crossing the Atlantic was interrupted by orders to join a large armada forming up in Norfolk. This was the major landing force for the invasion of North Africa. The fleet sailed under absolute radio silence and complete blackout conditions. We reached our assigned position for D-Day off the coast of Morocco on schedule. The destroyers took position close in to support the landing forces. When H-Hour arrived in the dark early morning hours, we were impressed by the giant shells, glowing like ingots passing over head, as the battleships and cruisers, further off shore, lobbed their projectiles toward targets on land.

Resistance was half-hearted and a few days later my ship was in Casablanca picking up supplies. On Christmas Day 1942 I was given the duty of leading a detail of petty officers on shore-patrol duty. Equipped with side-arms, rifles and Thompson sub-machine guns, we were sent to the *ancienne medina* quarter with the assignment of keeping sailors from "getting involved" with native women and perhaps precipitating an uprising. There were few incidents but we had a wonderful opportunity to see a part of Casablanca that looked much as it must have looked in biblical days. (We failed to stumble on Rick's nightclub or catch a glimpse of Ingrid Bergman or Humphrey Bogart, but we did see many individuals who could easily qualify as "the usual suspects.")

After North Africa my destroyer returned to its anti-submarine duties until we were ordered to take part in the landing in Sicily. We took position close in where we could deliver "called for" fire. Responding to instructions from spotters in the landing force, we were able to offer direct fire on enemy tanks and other strong points within four or five miles of the beach.

Near the end of 1943, as the submarine menace lessened, my ship was ordered to proceed to the South Pacific. We were to sail in company with the brand-new carrier, the U.S.S. *Franklin*. Heading south to Panama, the destroyer took its station in front of the carrier, sweeping back and forth across the track, hoping to intercept any submarine lying in wait. However, whenever the carrier conducted flight operations, we took station astern, ready to pick up the pilots of any planes that failed to make a safe landing on the flight deck.

No obstacles were encountered before reaching Panama. There, all hands held their collective breath as the carrier braced to squeeze through the canal. The new carriers had grown in size to a point where the only restriction on their size was the width of the three sets of locks that lifted transiting ships up and over the isthmian spine. The new ships were designed and built with only a few inches of clearance. When the *Franklin* was able to scrape through, we set course for Pearl Harbor and on to our respective assignments.

In the ensuing months my ship proceeded on "missions of war" to Eniwetok and on to Kwajalein, to the Admiralty Islands and New Guinea. As a unit alternately of the Third Fleet under Admiral Halsey and the Fifth Fleet under Admiral Spruance, we took part in a sequence of campaigns in the Marianas, the Palau Islands and the Philippines as American forces pushed the Japanese back to the home islands, culminating in the dropping of the bomb and the Japanese surrender. As a final Parthian shot, my ship carried a contingent of Marines into the Japanese naval base at Sasebo, Japan to begin the occupation.

With the war over, all thoughts turned to demobilization ... hopefully early demobilization. I felt rather confident since I had more separation points, based on length of service, than anyone else on the ship. However, we all had to accept the fact that no ship or other military unit could cripple itself by leaving necessary positions unfilled. It was not until early 1946 that a suitable replacement was found and I could turn toward home.

A native of Pasadena, Calif., Douglas graduated from Princeton University and spent his career in higher education. He also served as chairman of the Library Board and the Adult Education Board in Bronxville, N.Y. He and his wife Sally have a combined family of nine children.

View from the Bridge:
The Marshall Islands Invasions

Harold C. Moore Jr.

Harold C. Moore Jr.

The following account was recorded by Bill Askin, a sailor on board the U.S.S. LST 246 during the invasions of the Marshall Islands from January to September 1944. Mr. Askin was the Captain's Talker and kept a small notebook handy on the bridge to jot down notes and observances. His notes were later transcribed by Fred Friess. Harold "Chub" Moore, deceased husband of RiverMead resident Irene Moore, was an Ensign and Gunnery Officer on board during that time and received a copy of these notes provided to all crew members.

31 January 1944

U.S.S. *LST 246*: First U.S. ship to land on Jap territory: Kwajalien Atoll. General Quarters at 0627. Shell flashes all over horizons. Seem to be pounding hell out of them. One plane [flew] over at 0704, our own. We are separated from the convoy, moving slowly.

I first saw land through the long glass at 0715. Two small islands, heavily wooded. Quite a lot of ships all over. No air opposition at all. 13 Wildcats fly over in formation at 0718. Took first picture at 0745. Rain squall at same time. Aircraft over at various intervals. Two cans laying down heavy barrage on island. 0828 started moving up flank to join LST 243. Heavy bombardment still continuing. Island burning, heavy smoke all over. News of one small boat full of ammunition sunk.

0857: several explosions in succession as if oil tanks or ammo was going. Heavy fog all over, view hard. Took pic through long glass of can slapping shells at island. LCI's [Landing Craft, Infantry amphibious assault vessels] giving out with their rocket guns, said to fire 96 projectiles per minute. Pounding radio tower on Carlson

Island. Bombardment continuing on Carlos Island. [Our]Ship is in standby basis.

The Army has cleared the deck now. Bright sun with short intervals of rain. Landing proceeding amid fog and rain. G.O. secured at 1108. Can and battleship throwing plenty of heavy stuff at Porcelin. Dive bombers supporting. Several fires and one burning ship observed. Raining off and on still. First 'alligator' went off at 1225. Ordered to beach. The first of the LSTs. Beached hard on coral. Wire cage on island holding what is believed to be 17 natives from the island. Bombardment of Porcelin continues. Man killed under screws of small boat. He was on this ship ten minutes before it happened.

Pontoons were both off at 1818. Withdrew from beach at 1820 and beached by radio station at 1825. Duck aboard and first fully loaded one took to water at 1932. Ammunition continues going off. Two shells were fired at us as we beached; one going over our stern and one hitting 50 yards off our bow. Shrapnel from gun that blew up went all around ship.

1 February 1944

Artillery on Carlson, Enubuj and guns from cans, cruisers and battlewagons pounding Porcelin. Dive bombers pound heavy at 0850. DB's strafe beach and first wave of boats start moving at 0920.

0937: LCMs are seen moving toward beach. Shelling continues by land batteries as ships stop. Heavy fires on island. Beach as seen through glasses is utterly void of grass and trees. What trees are left are stripped by the guns.

One Navy plane was hit and burst into flames before hitting water. Six men killed on Carlson Island when gun blew up. Traces of lipstick, women's clothes found on Carlson. Good duty. Only one Jap was left on C.I. He was in a tree and shot one solder in the hand and was immediately made into a sieve. Rest evacuated to P.I. in small boats.

Shelling continuing. Troops on Porcelin progressing as planned at this time, 1408.

News aboard at 1622 is that casualties on both sides are heavy and there are 8,000 Japs on the island, which is many more than expected. About one-third of the island is in our possession. Flag raised on Carlson was flag from our ship (246).

2 February 1944

Shelling in morning not as heavy. Landings continue heavy. When gun blew up on Carlson the men were only injured. The Jap killed on Carlson had a very elaborate grave dug and even a tombstone.

Heard beach on Porcelin was hell, coral treacherous. Stopped boats 900 yards out in some cases. Later reports also indicated casualties on P.I. weren't as heavy as was believed. One observer on island said dead Japs were piled up like driftwood. Japs made counterattack on night of the 1st, but no details. Scuttlebutt of 20 Japs in small boats trying to land on C.I. to blow up radio tower; can discovered and destroyed. Steel in radio tower was very good steel, new steel.

Japs were preparing attack-proof defenses but here was a case of "too little, too late." Several Jap prisoners were taken to A.P.A. among them one woman in black.

We pulled off Beach 9890, unloaded and proceeded to lagoon side of Carlos Island. DD602, U.S.S. *Mead* came alongside and put empty shell casings aboard and took on five-inch shells from tank deck. Heard one BB [battleship] let go a salvo that hit our own troops and they, the BB, were told to cease firing and to get the hell away.

Moved remaining soldiers off our ship around 2000 to relieve infantry on beach. Fighting must be hard.

3 February 1944

Flash over the radio at 1145 said that the enemy was fleeing from the islands of Burton, Benson, Bennet and that destroyers were after them. They are going to move artillery from Carlson to Burton. Hospital ship relief moved past on way to Porcelin. One dead American was brought by small boat to be buried on Carlos. One Jap swam from P.I. to Carlson and surrendered; said that reinforcements were supposed to have arrived from Truk two days before we hit.

Aboard the cruiser *Indianapolis* on the 5th and talked with a crew member. Said they were shelling an island and one shell overshot the island, nearly blew the stern of the U.S.S *Louisville*, the *L* radioed back to the *Indianapolis* that they could have their shell back if they wanted it.

Casualties small on Porcelin. *LST 41* has holes in 16 tanks and is very low in the water at her bow. One LST, I think the *41*, has a broken eye-beam and is to be decommissioned.

One note on Porcelin: one girl had a baby when heavy shelling was going on. Said she was in terrible shape from concussion; no report on baby. Japs counterattacked four times in one night and met a solid curtain of steel laid down by the artillery on Carlson. Reports said most of the Japs were blown to pieces.

* * *

I slept topside night of the 9th and the stench of the dead Japs was terrific. Only have one foot of soil over their bodies.

* * *

Jap planes bombed and started large fires on Roi Island on the 12th of February. Read in the newspaper account that there were more Naval personnel in the invasion than in the whole U.S. Navy prior to December 7, 1941.

At this late date, 14 Feb, I learned that live Japs still on Porcelin. They are in underground tunnels and sneak out at night. The night of the 13th they killed four Americans.

Eniwetok Atoll

On way to Privilege. 0600 ran down an inter-island barge and sank it with 3 inch guns in a running battle.

17 February 1944

G.O. at 0600 and could see heavy cruisers shelling island. Shelling slow, no aircraft around, a few U.S. observation planes. Moved into lagoon through cleared channel. Very large concentration of ships in the lagoon. Reconnaissance going in on the artillery island at 1130.

We land on Camelia Island first. Two BBs heavily shelling Fragile Island, the one with the airstrip. Still no aircraft here; either enemy or friendly. Two BBs are the *Tennessee* and the *Pennsylvania* respectively. Also learned that BB *Washington* rammed BB *Indiana* putting the *Indiana* in dry dock. *Colorado* BB is in shelling. Watched two gators move into beach as two LCIs laid down a barrage of rocket fire and 40 mm plus 20 mms. No returning gunfire was seen.

We anchored off beach and first gator rolled off ramp at 1424. Island secured fast, nobody on it; just three huts. Three natives found on three islands. Lt. Col. in charge of Marines on ship was relieved of command for not getting his boys on the beach. Heard today, Feb. 19, that a sailor on LST off Fragile was shot through the jugular vein by a sniper on the island; sailor was on deck of his ship. Announced in yesterday's news that this atoll, Enitowek, was invaded. Heavy shelling now going on from Lady Slipper.

Japs on main island, Privilege, Enitowek, were reinforced with 1,000 more men two days before we arrived. Watched dive bombers bomb and strafe Parry and could see Japs firing back. Whole atoll secured at 1930 on the 22nd.

Landing on Privilege Island

Several small boat cox were killed going in; heavy losses and most got it right between the eyes.

The first six waves were all on the beach at the same time, side by side. Accurate mortar fire would have slaughtered them. They had to go over a slight hill and the Japs had continuous machine gun fire over this.

Password on beach was

> Q: Halt
> A: *January*
> Q: What month?
> A: *February*
> Q: Repeat
> A: *March*

One Jap walked up and when sentry said "Halt!" the Jap says "Friend, friend." Sentry laughed and said "friend my ass" and shot the hell out of him. Another Jap had it all right except on the command "repeat" he repeated, and they blasted him, too. One Jap officer came out of his fox hole, a canteen in one hand and a white flag in the other, crying for water. They cut him in half.

One native girl, they stripped her dress off and she started crying and wailing and quieted down immediately when they gave her a new one. She thought they were going to rape her like the Japs. A lot of the naked children were given the chocolate bars from the K Rations and they were eating it like chicken.

The burial squad was burying the Japs by the hundreds in holes dug by bulldozers. Dead Americans were wrapped in white canvas and taken by small boat to Lady Slipper and buried there.

Some soldiers said Privilege was worse than Tarawa. Snipers were getting over two Marines to one Jap. Snipers weren't in trees but at the base of the tree in very well camouflaged gun pits. A few Japs got in an officer's CP and wiped it out, officers and runners alike. American's own fire killed their own men. Whole atoll was supposed to be taken in 24 hours; it took 72 hours.

One pig on P. and when he was found he was the only body on the truck and they buried him separately. Tales told of arms, hands falling off or being broken off. Men using big packing hooks to drag them along.

Off Heart String, Parry, saw a fighter [plane] run head on into a 75mm shell and it blew up, flamed and crashed.

Another point about us and Parry. We were a decoy and merely put there so the Japs would open on us and expose their gun positions which, thank God, they did not fire. Later they did fire and put one shell on the wagon *Pennsylvania*, and put two on a LCI killing five and wounding 12 including all four officers on the latter.

When Roi was taken at Kwajalein the guns found there were Russian and British ones taken in the Crimean War.

New fact learned today, 1 March: when we entered Eniwetok Atoll we went directly over a minefield. If we had anything but a flat bottom... A mine sweep came in after us and dragged up 30 contact mines.

On way to Pearl on 5th. Can sweep dropped 18 depth charges. No result is known.

Third Invasion of Saipan in the Mariana Islands

15 June 1944

GQ at 0430. First saw island at 0510. Long, definitely an island. Not like Marshalls. Shelled it all night. Wagons laying in shells all along length of island. Air strip being pounded very heavily. Ocean crowded with ships. Radio reports all beaches favorable for landing. In other words, demolition did their job.

17 June 1944

This is definitely a hell of a lot worse than many of us anticipated. Although there is no Jap aircraft, ground forces are tough with latest in equipment and by far superiority in numbers (I heard we had 6,000 on beach to Japs' 12,000. You need 6-1 to invade.)

It was estimated that only 50 percent of each wave was making the beach. Mortar fire is terrific and accurate. Marines are unsure, or seem to be, and there is no sign of military organization from reports here.

On second day, Marines were beaten back and were forced to retreat clear to the beach and men from this ship lost practically everything. Army has gone on beach now and their style of fighting is needed, it seems.

Casualties are very heavy and now they are burying them at sea from *LST 218* and the *341*. Glad we weren't designated as hospital ship. Wounded men in boats pass by constantly, terrible to see.

Two Marines on board told of taking to a transport a Cee-Bee [Amphibious Construction Battalion] who had lost left leg, right arm and had his right leg shattered. He didn't know he had lost his leg and held the Marine's hand all the way.

Marines claimed that in another 15 minutes they would have cracked. Seabees and KIWIA (Marine CBs) and Army engineers trying to fix air strip are being picked off like flies. Say it is suicide to work there.

Last night on watch saw a gas dump blow sky high and when the concussion hit the ship it rocked like a can had fired over our fantail. Ten minutes later dirt and stones fell on the ship from the island; the flame was beautiful and awe-inspiring in the dusk, like a red flower bursting out.

Retreat on first night was very bad and a lot was lost. Heard story of one lieutenant in the Marines named Madden the boys swear by. Story goes a duck loaded with ammo was hit and set on fire. Everyone abandoned the duck and the lieutenant climbed in and had difficulty starting it. He had never driven one before he started it and drove it away from the men and then started unloading the burning ammo. Boys really liked his guts for that.

A sniper in a tree knocked off three Marines (deader 'n hell) before he got one through the stomach and fell from the tree. It was a Jap girl about 19 and she died on the hospital ship later (two hospital ships in here now, USS *Bountiful* and USS *Relief*).

Looked at town of Garapan through glasses and it has been heavily shelled. That is all except one house with Red Cross painted on it seems to have been missed entirely. Nice shooting!

At top point of island there are three large ships, two sunk and one seemingly afloat. One is supposed to be one of the President ships (*Coolidge*) that was captured at the outbreak of the war.

Saw my first dogfight Sunday (8th) and saw one man bail out in parachute. All up and down coral strip can be seen gators completely turned over and others deserted. Some ducks can be seen too, empty. When we launched our pontoons three men were hurt. Ship is having troubles on this trip, Wonder if it is the Skipper?

In grand total, we were under air attack nine times on return to Saipan. Jap prisoners all over and guarded by mean looking Negro soldiers who were giving Japs hell. One barn housed about seven cattle who seemed perfectly happy.

They say that snipers still come out of the hills. Some very bizarre stories. On board two small Jap ships and saw enemy logs written in English (parts) Very dirty ship though.

Could see seaplane hanger and field. One plane wrecked on strip and hanger stripped. Passed sunken ships, one was U.S., ex mine- sweep, probably from Guam, all ripped open. Other ships looked like a sieve. Jap women working on air strip for 25 cents a day and laughing at the men working too.

Invasion of Peleliu Island- Palau Group
15 September 1944

Notes on way: Trip will take 11 days. Only GQ to be rung will be the real thing. Air protection full way. Between 1700 and 1800 on 10 September felt six depth charges, later learned sub was hit.

Got dope on island and here is what I know on D-Day Minus 4: Island is 2 miles by 5 miles with a very good fighter strip (mean Bomber) made up in X style and extends practically to the beach. There will be three beaches, White 1 and 2, Orange 1,2,3 and Scarlet 1,2, and 3. We will beach on Orange 1. Three of our LVT will be in the first wave. Our two small boats will take in the 4th and 8th waves.

LCI(M) are being used for the first time out here. M standing for mortar. About five of these plus your rocket firing LCIs.

It is expected to work night fighters off the strip by the second night. Indications point to a week of bombing by the Japs after D Day. At least, that is what they expect.

We will let off LVIs, etc. from LST Area Baker, approximately five miles out. This is the closest of the big ships, however. From point of operations, we will be within bombing range of 81 Jap air strips including bomber strip on Luzon, P.I.

Met other convoy on night of 14th. All transports, LCIs and cans.

News tells of heavy bombing for four days now. Still have planes overhead. Very calm sea for three days now, no roll at all. It is the calm before the storm. Sky overcast on night before D-Day. Intermittent gun flashes on horizon, the big babies.

D-Day. First saw island at 0535, very low like Marshall Islands. Other small islands to left as we approach. Shellfire off to the right. Smoke on island. Weather perfect. On first look through glasses, island is heavily vegetated but wagons seem to be leveling it off. On the right side of island it appears like machine-gun fire is hitting the water. Spurts of water can be seen. No aircraft of either side, saw only float plane.

0655 bow doors open and ramp down. Both small boats in water. 0718 first vehicle off. All 18 off at 0726. Reports at 0945 say the beach is very rugged, very very...Several Amtraks [Assault Amphibious Vehicles] can be seen burning. Using a lot of the new phosphorus shells that are supposed to create a vacuum when they explode and suck all the air out.

LCIs giving island merry hell. Island heavily overcast with smoke. Fighting rugged, 15th wave called from the beach and told 16th not to come in because of heavy fire. One officer who went to beach, making this his 4th, said mortar fire was heaviest yet. One LCT went in and unloaded five tanks and as they went into the water they picked them all off right down the row. Japs got two of our planes. One boat took in 12 D.U.K.W.s [amphibious vehicles also known as "duck boats"] and four came back out. The other eight?? One LST (*661*) got stuck on the beach and was under heavy fire.

D+2 (Sunday): Island fighting going slow...are practically flattening out the hill on the island. Army landed on Anguar and appear to be going good. Our ship moved into beach and binoculars told story. First time I've ever seen tank traps by Japs. Long branches stuck up in rows all over the beach. Several D.U.K.W.s burned to a crisp, one smashed entirely.

Watched dive bombers come in, let go and zoom upward, strafing plans coming in later. Still excites you to watch them come in.

Cruiser *Denver* is here throwing in the shells and also the wagon *New Jersey*. Watched one LCI (*456*) move in and let rockets go on beach. These babies pack power plus terrific racket and damage too and then it followed up with 40 and 20 mm fire. Saw two dead bodies, horrifying is the word for it. One face down with only pants on and the other all bloated. Practically unrecognizable as a former human being. "We regret to inform you..."

One of our boats took in Paramount newsreel cameramen, among who was ex-actor Bill Lundigan who was sporting a beard. He was wounded later. Boys said there were cameramen all over the place.

LST 271 is a hospital ship and every morning at 0800 it buries its dead over the side in canvas with chains. Pushed over 15.

On D-Day the 1st, second, third and fourth waves all combined into one and hit together. Using rocket planes on this deal, that is, planes carrying rockets (so I ain't neat).

Pontoons off at 1340, D-Day plus two. 1407 saw mortar fire off beach and then suddenly the beach emptied of all men, leaving in boats, amtraks, anything. The cry of "gas" had gone off. Some men came aboard with burns but it can't be said it was gas. It was remarkable how that beach emptied.

Several mortars were fired at ship, wounding one of the ships company (Becker). I was back by the fantail with the 20 mm [guns] with about 15 Marines and we all ducked. No heroes here...no need of any.

In close to Jap-held beach and could see machine gun bullets reaching out for us ($6.40 seats).

Got the dope on massacre of first waves; Japs let them get on beach and move in and then they put artillery fire behind them and moved it up, thus trapping them. Whole companies were wiped out. Only 2-5 men came back out of various companies. Tarawa looks sick next to this deal.

Stories: One Jap tank was mixed up and ran onto an American beach and the boys were shooting everything at it and it was going all over like mad.

140 Geisha girls were captured...bull!

Rumor flying all over the beach is "Germany has surrendered" and "MacArthur hits Phillipines." Both fake but there were firm believers. One CP signaled out and asked confirmation. Rumor at Saipan was "Russia declared war on Japan"

On the air strip could be seen several wrecked Jap planes painted gray with red sun on side. Wrecked hangers and buildings glimpsed too.

Learned that a Jap destroyer was surprised here and made a run for it. Out cans caught it and sunk it. 40 survivors picked up and put on USS *Windsor*. Only 1 prisoner had been taken on D Day plus 2, an officer.

Cases have been found where Geisha girls were found in the shell holes with the men side by side.

One Marine had a booklet, Japanese, that had photos of Jap victories, surrender of Corregidor, carrier sinkings, etc.

Learned story on "mortar fire" from island. It was shell fire from a US-made 105mm! Japs captured it with six shells and threw them all at the 246.

Two of the Jap bombers on the airstrip were C-54 Douglas Sky Transports in Jap paint. Japs using railway guns here as in Saipan.

Fire from open fissure on cliff and recoil shoved them in cliff after round, short track.

Army, after securing Anguar, was called in to help Marines and the doggies really rubbed it in.

The best story going the rounds now is a beaut. Seems some Marines had some Japs trapped in a cave, then all of a sudden about ten Japanese women walked out. All were gorgeous, built perfect and, of course, entirely nude. They walked toward the Marines offering all when one Marine, the story goes, saw Jap soldiers creeping up behind so the gallant lads opened up and wiped all out, women and soldiers. That is a story.

The Island was a training base for Imperial Marines. Warehouses were found stacked with uniforms. Helluva boot camp if you ask me.

Dead Jap floated by ship on the 28th, wearing only sandals, face down, all bloated and within a hundred feet. We beached at noon on the 25th and damned near broke off the bow door (port side).

This is my account as I saw it from the bridge of the U.S.S. *LST 246*.

The Captain's Talker, Bill Askin, Y 2/C

THE DAY WE HIT THE MINE

WIN NELSON

Sometimes our memories of an experience such as World War II tend to focus on one incident. For me, it was the day our minesweeper (*YMS 41*) exploded a mine right under its keel. We were one of 38 YMS minesweepers assigned to clear the harbor at Balikpapan, Borneo, an important oil center held by the Japanese. General MacArthur and the Australians were to invade there on July 1, 1945. Allied airmen had dropped more magnetic and acoustic mines off Balikpapan harbor than anywhere in the southwest Pacific.

The day was Thursday, June 28, 1945. Because of the danger of mine explosion, all of us were to be on deck continually during sweeping operations. No one was below decks. At 1405, we hit a mine. Along with seven others from our crew of 35, I was thrown into the air and landed in that warm water with only minor wounds. We lost no lives. One of my shipmates, Dennahy, dove in. He swam over to check on all eight of us who were floating in the harbor. (During sweeping, we all wore our lifejackets.) In time, a rescue craft picked us up. We were brought aboard the cruiser *Colombia* where our wounds were tended.

Well, there you have it! But you know, I will never forget that feeling of being suddenly thrust up into the air, then being underwater and finally coming to the surface. I believed that God was with me. I tried to calm Loftus, my shipmate in the water. He was sure sharks would get us. All of us were glad when Dennahy swam out to help us.

The Navy determined to save our minesweeper. They sent divers to come and cut off 30 feet of our fantail (the stern). Then other workers came to cement up the exposed area of our stern.

Meanwhile, V-J day arrived! What to do with this YMS, or the remaining three-quarters of a ship? By that time, we had been towed to Moratai in the Netherlands East Indies. Someone somewhere cooked up a plan which involved our being towed further: 1,600 miles all the way to Samar Island in the Philippines. That was another week I will never forget: The tug, using a one-half inch cable, planned to tow two large metal barges and us (all in a line) the full 1,600 miles. En route, the cable parted between the barges. For one whole day we were adrift, surrounded by sharks. Luckily, one seaman, a former professional fisherman, caught a six foot sand shark. That night we had fresh seafood for dinner.

A month after arriving at Samar, we were ordered to decommission our ship. She rests now on the bottom of Manicani Harbor. A wooden vessel built at the Bath Iron Works in Bath, Maine, in 1938, she travelled halfway round the world and earned her rest.

I came back from this whole experience grateful as never before just to be alive. I had always wanted to be a minister; now the call was louder and clearer.

The return to Harvard (after one summer term in 1943) was a most exhilarating time. It involved being in the band, getting engaged to Lynn and moving on to three more years at Yale Divinity School.

As I think about my life, I am reminded of what an elderly lady in tennis shoes once said as she stood in line at a healing conference: "Life is like going down a river jumping from one raft to another. It is truly the grace of God that brings us through." I really think of ours not so much as "the greatest generation" but rather the "stand-together generation". And I hope our stand together today is for peace and justice for all.

Born in Hartford, Conn., Win graduated from the Loomis School, Harvard College and the Yale Divinity School. He served as a minister in Congregational churches (United Church of Christ) in Maine, Connecticut, Minnesota and New Hampshire. He and his wife, Beryl (Lynn), have three children.

Tough Duty

Donald M. Sherk

You speak fluent English. I think you would make a good sailor, sonny. Would you like to be in the Navy? Come back tomorrow.

Those were the words of the recruiting officer when I was drafted in January 1945 after graduating from the Mount Hermon School. Actually I had been chauffeured to Grenier Field in Manchester, N.H., by the mother of the late Walter Peterson (former Governor of New Hampshire) to be inducted into the Army with a group from northern New Hampshire. "Luck of the draw" or whatever, I returned the next day as instructed and enlisted in the Navy. Initially assigned to boot camp at Sampson, N.Y., I was transferred to electrician's school at Great Lakes, Ill.

At Great Lakes, I came down with scarlet fever and following recovery had some trouble with my eyes. Naval "wisdom" dictated that I be assigned to a large ship that had an optical shop that could grind lenses. But Naval needs trumped wisdom and, equipped with six pair of naval-issue eyeglasses, I was assigned for duty aboard a small mine sweeper operating off the West Coast.

"Chasing" that mine sweeper involved assignment to the Navy base at Camp Shoemaker and Treasure Island in Oakland Bay. The train trip there from Great Lakes was interrupted by frequent stops but made more interesting by the warm welcomes of the USO stations along the way offering coffee, food and encouragement.

On New Year's Eve in San Francisco, a "well-heeled" family was looking for a couple of service personnel to help celebrate the occasion. A friend and I volunteered without hesitation. We were picked up by a chauffeur and driven to a penthouse apartment with a private elevator located at the top of Nob Hill. After a delicious dinner served by a wait staff and an evening of dancing with the couple's daughter and friend, we were presented with food and gifts and chauffeured back to our base. Apparently our host was president of a very large company.

Meanwhile, I was a "sailor in waiting" for that mine sweeper. My responsibility was to muster every morning at 9 a.m. The rest of the day I could enjoy sports, movies and relaxation. It was tough duty. As it turned out, the ship I had been waiting for had been given to the British several months earlier.

Finally I was assigned to a ship operating out of Puget Sound on the northwest coast. Our mission was to patrol the waters of the west coast. That ocean may be called the 'Pacific' but I have never been so seasick.

At the end of the war, I returned home, enrolled at Keene State under the GI Bill and graduated with a bachelor's degree from the University of New Hampshire. That was followed by a master's degree in education from the University of Connecticut and a career in education.

Born in Teheran, Persia, Don grew up in Brecksville, Ohio, and attended Brecksville High School, Mount Hermon School, and the University of New Hampshire before earning his Masters at the University of Hartford. He was a teaching principal and fifth- and sixth-grade teacher in Mansfield, Wethersfield and Hartford, Conn., and in the ConnVal School District in New Hampshire. He and his wife Shirley have two children.

"Wonders" in the Pacific

Cal Sholl

"—you will proceed to San Diego, California and the Commandant, Eleventh Naval District for active duty afloat — "

After enlisting in the Navy's V-12 program and following three months of midshipman's school, those were the orders that sent me to sea. The V-12 program called for an adjustment in my courses with emphasis on math and physics but allowed for the completion of a junior year with on-campus training by a group of gutsy marine sergeants - a major cultural change. Midshipman's school was on the shores of Lake Champlain in Plattsburg, N.Y. We were the first Navy class to take over this old army base. With a frozen lake, one 60-foot power boat, inadequate furnishings and outdated equipment, it was an unlikely venue for training what became known as the Navy's "ninety day wonders".

We thought the Navy was "enlightened" when they had us spend a few minutes with a "shrink" and asked what our duty preference would be after getting our commissions. I opted for duty aboard a destroyer. Preference apparently was not part of the calculation. With the same orders directed to Sholl, Shotwell and Silver, it was clear that groups were picked alphabetically and randomly assigned. "Duty afloat" could mean a landing craft or a carrier and anything in between. The only thing we could be sure of was that we would be on the water.

In San Diego, duty afloat was not immediate. There were a few weeks of monitoring communications from battle areas in the Pacific, training in firefighting and damage-control exercises. In my wildest dreams I could not have imagined an assignment as second officer aboard a 130-foot sailing schooner, but those were my orders. The Navy had confiscated this beautiful vessel named *Enchantress* to be used by a group of scientists from the University of California division of war research doing sound experiments. They did not want any interference from propulsion equipment so we were to sail. That was great except for the fact that sailing had not been included in our 90- day training curriculum. We had a skipper who had all of four months of experience at sea, a crew of half a dozen enlisted personnel and a handful of scientific wizards.

Heading out of the bay at San Diego and passing through the antisubmarine net at Point Loma was fulfilling my aspiration for "duty afloat," albeit not aboard a destroyer. We were under power with a small auxiliary engine capable of providing a top speed of about six knots. As the junior officer I had the night watch. It was pitch black – no moon, no stars. Although west-coast blackouts had been eased by that time, there was no trace of a shoreline visible. Our dead-reckoning course took us close to a light house on the point of San Clemente Island. The skipper's instructions were to make sure we were well to the starboard of that light. At about the time we estimated we should see the beacon, there it was flickering on the horizon. All was well. But as a seaman and I stood on the bow, another brighter flicker appeared. This made no sense at all until a whole string of lights came into view. Apparently all was not well. I was convinced we were headed for some beach and ordered "all engines stop - full reverse - wake up the skipper - be ready for grounding!" By then we were surrounded by "lights" - the phosphorescence created by a tremendous school of fish frolicking in the calm waters of the Pacific. So here was this "ninety-day wonder" who could not tell the difference between a light house and a school of fish.

The next day we ran into a heavy squall. With our decks awash, the wind howling in the rigging and my head buried in a bucket, I longed for that beach I thought we were headed for the night before. Again, it was not my finest hour.

When we reached our "station," we found we were to work with a newly commissioned submarine. The scientists wanted the sub to make passes at a hydrophone that we trailed from the fantail. The sub was to start several hundred yards away and gradually close to a "near miss" on the final pass. Meanwhile, the scientists experimented with their array of sound equipment trying to differentiate between the sounds of whales and subs. It was a boring day and all of us were relieved when the time came for the final run. The sub approached slowly as planned at periscope depth but instead of veering to starboard, it passed right under us with periscope and conning tower hitting the deep keel of our vessel. We suffered a significant jolt but no real damage. When the sub did an emergency surfacing routine nearby, it was evident that its periscope was badly damaged.

That episode soon became the main topic of conversation which relieved me of hearing about lights and schools of fish. We speculated that the sub's skipper had given an order for "left" instead of "right full rudder" and in so doing had earned a desk job for the remainder of the war. Knowing that a supposedly experienced captain could make that kind of mistake made me feel just a tad better about my school of fish episode.

Duty aboard the *Enchantress* was interrupted by new orders. The luck of the draw and alphabetical position sent me to Tacoma, Wash., to join the crew of a newly constructed refrigerated cargo vessel. It was actually a 128-foot tuna clipper. The Navy had found these vessels to be ideal for supplying advance bases in the South Pacific. They had a history of dealing with heavy weather and had the capacity to hold 300 tons of frozen foods as well as 25,000 gallons of diesel fuel, allowing for long-range operations. The only modification for wartime use was the addition of four 20mm anti-aircraft guns. Navigation equipment consisted of a magnetic compass and a sextant. It was far removed from being a destroyer but I could be thankful it was not a landing craft destined for invasion of some south Pacific atoll.

I was the junior of three officers. The skipper and the "exec" were LT (jg)s with less than six months of sea duty. A few of the incidents that follow may be memorable but not momentous. They do provide a feeling for "duty afloat" and the contribution of at least a few of the Navy's "ninety day wonders" in the backwaters of the South Pacific where we were marginally prepared, inadequately equipped but well fed. Others, less fortunate, have harrowing tales of courage and sacrifice that make for much more interesting reading.

Our voyage to the South Pacific took us first to San Pedro, Calif., where we were briefed on our route to the Philippine Islands and provisioned for the trip. One night on the way down the coast we were "challenged" by a signal light from a shore battery. Although we had the proper code signal response we were inexperienced at sending Morse code by a signal light and an impatient artillery unit was poised to eliminate the "enemy" until an experienced signalman (aroused from sleep) saved our hides at the last minute - another example of "wonders" at work.

At our top speed of ten knots, a small convoy escorted us to Hawaii on a prescribed zig-zag course intended to thwart submarine attack. This leg of the journey was marred only by a malfunction of our main engine causing us to be dead in the water for half a day — a somewhat risky position for the convoy. At Pearl Harbor a blown ammonia compressor gasket caused an abandon-ship exercise that was real — not a practice drill. Fortunately we were dockside in the harbor at the time and the only casualty was a mascot mutt that we honored with a proper burial at sea.

We joined a smaller convoy to Kwajalien atoll where there was evidence of a hard-fought battle to secure the atoll. From there we proceeded to Leyte Gulf in the Philippine Islands. The logic of sending us alone (no convoy) on this leg escaped us but those were the orders. The boredom of the voyage was relieved somewhat by the challenge of celestial navigation using a sextant on the deck of a rolling and pitching small ship. Finding a true horizon was almost impossible and our plotted positions were questionable. Other distractions involved practice with the 20mm anti-aircraft guns, general quarters and damage control drills, rare sightings of what appeared to be periscopes, viewing an incendiary bomb headed for our west coast, dealing with sudden squalls and watching water spouts, studying U.S. Armed Forces Institute correspondence courses and writing letters home.

We arrived at Leyte Gulf as if being led by the hand. That was one of the miracles of the war. The crew was convinced that three inexperienced reservists could never find their way to dry land after sailing over 2,500 miles of the Pacific using just a magnetic compass and sextant.

The rest of the tour was spent supplying remote bases located in places like Borneo, Cebu, Samar and Mindanao. All of these ports were fairly well secured by the time we got there but surrounding areas were still infested by Japanese with a "kamikaze" intent. Typhoons may have been more of a threat to us and there was one night in Surigao Strait when every one of us was desperately seasick and would have welcomed being blown ashore.

The mantra of Pacific forces was "Golden Gate in 48." One afternoon in early August of 1945 we heard an unbelievable broadcast about a "super bomb" being dropped on Japan. The events that followed prompted a celebration in Leyte Gulf beyond any Fourth of July fireworks display. The saga of this "tuna clipper" is in sharp contrast to the stories of the fighting Navy and those who were in harm's way. However, it provides some insight as to the support provided to the real heroes of the war. Some of us were lucky. Others really deserve to have their stories told and to be honored for their sacrifice.

Tarnished gold braid was a sign of having been at sea. A little experience earned a tad more respect enhanced by promotion in grade level. I was feeling like an "old salt" now able to at least tell the difference between a light beacon and a school of fish.

I was also anxious to get home which was dependent on a point system that focused on length of service, grade level, dependents and availability of a replacement. In late January of 1946 I had the necessary points to get out and quickly arranged passage on a troop ship returning to the States. Sailing under the Golden Gate Bridge two years earlier than expected was a joy not dampened in the least by any misgivings regarding atomic bombs. That would be a subject to ponder later when the chemistry of maturity fostered a more objective global view of the new nuclear era and a world still in conflict.

A native of Pitman, N.J., Cal graduated from Bucknell University and earned his MBA at Syracuse University. He worked in industry and management consulting throughout his career. He and his wife Nancy have four children. He volunteered for a wide range of civic, professional and charitable organizations.

A Ticket To See the World

Arthur L. Stevenson

My wartime experience can only be characterized as education - in all the many facets of life about which I knew next to nothing. I was never shot at by an enemy. Before entering into active duty in the Army Air Force, I had never spent a night outside of Massachusetts. My stateside active duty assignments took me to Boca Raton, Fla., Yale University in New Haven, Conn., Tomah, Wisc., Galveston, Tex., and Washington State. My overseas duty took me to Oahu and Maui in the Hawaiian Islands, to Guam and Saipan in the Marianas and finally to Iwo Jima.

I entered Williams College as a freshman in September of 1941 and the country was at war less than three months later. The college immediately went on an accelerated academic schedule, with reduced vacation time and classes running from seven o'clock in the morning until late afternoon. The draft authorities offered deferred status until we had completed four semesters of college provided we enlisted immediately in one of the services. My choice was the Army Air Force. It was an easy choice; the alternative was to go on active duty immediately.

I received active duty orders in May 1943 and ultimately was trained as an Intercept Fighter Controller, directing fighter aircraft in interception of enemy aircraft by use of radar plots and air-ground radio communication with the fighter squadrons. When our unit finally got to Guam in the Marianas, the Japanese air force had almost ceased to exist, and our work then became that of directing and controlling air-sea rescue of downed B-29 bomber crews of the 20th Air Force.

When the war finally ended in the Pacific, I spent an unconscionable time getting home because I had limited service, no wife, no dependents and no particular reason why anyone should hasten my homecoming. I ultimately returned to the United States and was mustered out at Fort Dix, N.J., in August 1946 with the rank of Captain.

I am grateful for my military experience because of what it taught me about life, the world and other people. Through the G.I. Bill (one of the great legislative acts of this country), I was able to accumulate enough credits to get through college.

In a spasm of patriotism, I had signed up for the Air Force Reserve in 1946 (when I was released from active duty) and was called back to active duty during the Korean War in September 1950, when I was just starting my third year in law school. This hitch was a total waste of time because the ground tactical control equipment we were supposed to be using was still on the drawing boards. However, during the seventeen months of Korean War service, I accumulated further G. I. Bill credits so that I graduated from Harvard Law School in 1953 with a fine education and no student debt.

I believe we should require some form of national service from our young people, whether it be military or civilian (like the old Civilian Conservation Corps of the F.D.R. years). I grew up and learned a lot from 1943 to 1946 and there is no other way I could have duplicated this part of my education.

Born in Boston, Mass., Arthur spent many years as a resident of Concord, Mass. A graduate of Williams College and Harvard Law School, he worked as an attorney in Boston for most of his career, and as a trust investment advisor for eleven years. He served in town government, having been a selectman, town counsel and moderator. He and his wife Margaret, who have two children, were named Honored Citizens of Concord in 2001.

The War in Photos

December 7, 1941: The Day that Will Live in Infamy. Front page of the New York Herald Tribune *announces the beginning of hostilities for the United States. Courtesy Chris Kelly, whose story begins on Page 201.*

Below, a view of the carnage during the sneak attack on Pearl Harbor. Courtesy Cal Sholl, Page 155.

Although Arthur Stevenson looks here like a wizened veteran of numerous island invasions, in fact he never saw combat during the war, nor when he was called back for duty in Korea. His story can be found on Page 160.

U.S.S. LST 246 *participated in numerous invasions and landings throughout the Marshall Islands and elsewhere in the Pacific. The Captain's Talker day-by-day log of events begins on Page 139.*

Some of the "90-day Wonders" attending Midshipman's School prior to being commissioned and sent off to their ships in the Pacific. Courtesy Cal Sholl. Story Page 155.

He wanted to serve on a destroyer, but instead Cal Sholl was assigned to this 128-foot former tuna clipper to supply advance bases across the Pacific. Story, Page 155.

Timeline of World War II Events ★ ★ 165

LST 246 *heads for an unnamed beach during one of the Marshall Island invasion actions. Harold "Chub" Moore Jr. was an officer on the ship. Story begins on Page 139.*

David Clinkenbeard served in a M.A.S.H. unit in Korea, flying injured soliders in helicopters and doing occasional artillery recon in fixed-wing planes like the one above. His story is found on Page 119.

PART THREE:
The Home Front
The Victory Garden

George L. Andersen

In 1942 there was a need for accurately scaled plane models to train the plane spotters that protected us from enemy aircraft. My friends and I were students at Woodrow Wilson Junior High in Philadelphia and many of us had built models and were eager to help the cause. The school was helpful in getting specifications and about eight of us started to work, some at home and some in the shop that the school allowed us to use.

It became obvious that each of us had different skills and while our individual models were acceptable, we could improve our output with a better division of labor. The government had provided the incentive of a certificate for the completion of an impressive number of models and we were, as well, anxious to do our little bit to aid the war effort. Most boys reach the highest ratio of warrior spirits to ability at this age. We decided to pool our efforts and share the Certificates evenly, and divided the work for about ten identical models and proceeded with operations.

I did the first carving of each fuselage because this was a skill I had developed by carving many pieces of balsa wood in making models that I had also designed. Most of the others had built from somewhat pre-carved kits. Others prepared wings, elevators, or tail fins because they were good at working the wood in thin sections while staying accurately to scale.

After a joint inspection we assembled the planes, added fillers, sanded and finished them with a coat of the specified dull-gray paint. The result was ten planes of the same quality in less time, so we worked the same way from then on. I don't recall any issues about Certificate distribution, but I suspect that each of us felt satisfied that we had contributed "a little more than average" in a helpful role in the war effort.

We were happy to have the value of our efforts demonstrated in an extraordinary event that, according to my foggy memory, took place on Long Island. A woman spotter, trained with the use of models like ours, reported seeing a Japanese Zero. Her superiors were skeptical, and even the press made fun of the poor soul who believed that Zeros had a range that included the East Coast. She was exonerated when the Air Corps confirmed that they had test flown a captured Zero as part of their evaluation of enemy aircraft capabilities.

Our most rewarding experience came when a representative of the Air Corps came to the school for a meeting with the principal, the teacher who oversaw our model-making and all the model makers. He first congratulated us for what we had done, which he said had qualified us for a unique and secret new assignment. He made us promise not to reveal any aspect of the models we were to build. Further, the principal agreed to lock up all plans in the safe each night along with the work itself. Secrecy ensured, he then laid out the plans.

To this day I remember my thoughts when I first saw a scale drawing of what was clearly a giant plane. Even though I was looking at a piece of paper about 30 by 40 inches, it seemed the largest thing I had ever seen. It was the B-19 bomber. Larger than the B-17 by far, we were awed. As we built the models, we were especially pleased that the student body knew that we were working on a secret, and therefore important, project. The more secret we kept it, the more important it appeared. The government of the time was wise in using the skills of such young volunteers. I wonder if a current group of kids would have such imagination and common sense. Further, I have for years worried that modern youngsters are not nearly as interested in model planes. It was a great help in my later career as an engineer. I doubt that computer games or television has the same educational value.

Our Victory Garden

One example of necessity and invention was when "organic" gardening technology made a breakthrough in 1942; and two small boys in the heart of Philadelphia turned rats into seeds.

The voice on the radio said it was the duty of citizens to have a "Victory Garden." Around the corner from our house was a vacant lot, with a row of houses being built nearby. The builders always had a trash heap which they periodically burned. From this we were able to rescue sticks and string to make a fence. My brother and I staked out a large garden on the clearest, flattest portion of the lot. We had just started digging when the trouble started.

We had not been alone in hearing the call for "Victory Gardens." Men came out of the houses in droves, but found the prime space for a garden already occupied by two small but energetic boys. The men explained that we could never garden that large a space. This was true but we did not see that then. After some discussion, we reached a compromise appropriate to our station in life. Our stakes were removed and dumped in a small heap. The clear, flat garden area was neatly divided into plots which the men promptly started to till.

Some of the families whose houses backed onto the lot had always had gardens there. They "squatted," so to speak, by extending their back yards onto the lot. One of the men who had such a garden plot was ancient, knowledgeable and sympathetic. A tall, spare man, I noticed him watching our contretemps with the men. I fleetingly thought that he might come to help, as he was always friendly. But he just watched and then called us over.

He asked, "Why did you choose that spot anyway?" We pointed out that it was flat and clear and therefore the easiest place to garden. "Why do you think that area is so clear?" He was like that; he asked questions all the time. I don't remember how many more questions he needed before we realized the truth of the situation. We had just been evicted from the most barren land on the block. Mr. Socrates suggested that we put our garden next to "The Dump."

The dump was literally a hole in the ground. Many years before, it may have been very deep. It was round, roughly a hundred feet in diameter, and had been partially filled with broken concrete. Over the years, trash and grass cuttings and leaves had built up, but it was still a substantial depression which always had at least some standing water. It didn't always smell good.

We considered our friend's advice since, as a man who had retired from business but not from life, he always had a beautiful garden. We knew that he was right about the barren land. But we also saw that there were other areas where the weeds grew well. Besides, near the dump the soil was full of broken concrete and rusty cans.

We compromised. We staked out an area not far from the dump where the weeds were tall. Actually, they were taller than we were, but we knew just what to do. Just like the builders; when you have something you don't want, burn it.

We set fire to the weeds. At first, our plan worked well. Then too well. Then ... well!! Mr. S. and a number of other men came to our rescue. One of them brought a large canvas drop cloth. Two men pulled this slowly over the edge of our fire, smothered most of the flames, and brooms and shovels handled the rest. Soon the fire was out, but a far larger area was now clear than we had planned.

Some over-excitable adult had called the police. We chatted. Actually it was not exactly a two way conversation. These kind gentlemen even gave us a ride. They initially indicated that our destination was the hoosegow. While we worried about that, they actually drove us home, where we were given the opportunity of explaining the situation to our parents. It was a few days before we could return to our garden. But there was no "our garden" to return to. After we had cleared the land, a second brigade of adults had come and seized all that was arable. All that was left was the slope of the dump. We talked to our friend, Mr. S. He examined the area and pronounced it ideal, except for two things. One, we had to plan to avoid erosion on the slope. Second, there were rats in the dump.

We brought out our shovels and started working. It's hard to dig when the soil is a mixture of concrete chunks, cans, dirt and compost. With a pick and crow bar, we dug out the rocks and concrete chunks and threw them into the water. Our father helped us build a giant sifter. It was a a wooden frame rack with a wire-mesh bottom. Set at an angle to the ground, it was taller than we were. We now threw the mixture of glass, cans, dirt and compost at the top of the screen. The larger bits slid down the screen and were thrown into the dump; while under the rack a pile of soil accumulated.

I had always loved to read, and devoured all the books at our library on farming and gardening. One of the things I read about was the terrace farming in China and I can still see the pictures in the book in my mind's eye. Mr. S had alerted us to the erosion potential of our site, so we created mini terraces with small stones and boards from the builder's waste pile, and filled each with dirt and compost. The longest row of vegetables we ever had was about four feet.

Our garden took shape. Actually it assumed quite an odd shape. Picture a giraffe that lost a battle with a steam roller. We had planned a perfect rectangle of 100 x 50 feet. We ended with a classic gerrymander. It was about 40 feet long and varied in width from six to fifteen feet. It turned out to be the perfect size.

Our allowances would not cover our planned purchases of seed and plants. That's when we transmuted rats into seeds! When you garden in the country, you worry about rabbits and groundhogs. In the city you worry about rats. Ours was not a rat-infested area, but there are always sewer rats. Also, our dump was an ideal rat abode. The initial fill of broken concrete had created a built-in underground tunnel network. We discovered that our dog, Rex, was a natural born ratter. We were prying up a large rock in the garden, when a rat shot out from underneath and dashed toward the water. He didn't get four feet! The rat quickly exited this world, and Rex dropped the body with a proud finality. We told Mr. S. about this. He was more than pleased, and gave us a "bounty" payment. As did the other gardeners whenever we killed rats. So when my brother and I needed money for the garden, we had only to turn over some rocks and let Rex do his thing. We were sorry when we ran out of rats, although the other men weren't. But we had our seeds and plants for the first season.

The men around us were working enthusiastically, and also buying every product advertised for the "Victory Garden." This included fertilizer. We decided we needed some fertilizer too and because we were flush with two rats-worth of funds, we visited the hardware store to buy some. Rats! We discovered that fertilizer would cost us three rats-worth!

Of course, in 1942, an excellent source of fertilizer was free in Philadelphia. The milkman and other vendors still used horses for deliveries, and the horse-made fertilizer was often free for the taking. I think this was the point at which my brother retired from agriculture. The only competition for the product was from the sparrows. Though numerous they were not well organized. That was source one.

Source two? I had a friend with a pigeon coop. He had always thrown away his charge's awful offal. From Mr. S., I learned that this particular product would need substantial dilution. Happily, just at the edge of our plot, there was an old, rusty 55-gallon drum. It was mostly buried, and in a nearly vertical position. I was able to dig out its contents, except for the water. Because of the high water table there, it was always partially filled. Just what we needed. Each week I threw in some pigeon manure which mixed with the water. Just before adding the horse manure, I dipped out buckets of "aged sauce" and watered the plants. Total manure cost: ZERO. Results: the healthiest plants in the block.

The healthy plants looked good to me, and to the droves of predatory bugs. My reading had shown that nicotine was an ingredient of many insecticides. Also, I learned that soap was used to make sure any insecticide wetted the plant and adhered properly. My father smoked, as did most of the adult male population. So there was no problem in making cigarette tea.

I soaked tobacco from donated butts in water. Then with a little added soap, I sprayed the mixture on any plant that had bugs. All this worked well enough and the plants grew apace. Even with a much smaller area than planned, the output was such that we had a substantial surplus. We imitated the hucksters and sold those items from our wagon. For years our mother said, "Those kids fed half the neighborhood.".

Our garden was a "Victory!"

To this day, I am a happy gardener. It has much to commend it. For instance, one practices humility while turning the manure pile, and the connection to growing things is soothing to the spirit. I think we may be closest to heaven with our fingers in the earth. Weeds excepted!

After his service, George graduated from Widener University in 1951 and earned his Masters from Haverford in 1954. He spent his career in science and engineering and is the holder of some 20 patents. He served on numerous civic, professional and community boards. A native of Philadelphia, Pa., George was married to Joan for 48 years and Patricia for four and has two children.

Our Lives Would Never Be the Same

Bailey Arthur

My memories and stories of WW II begin before the war in the small town of Canton, Mass., located in the shadow of Blue Hill, the highest point of land along the New England coast. I was born in Canton and had three siblings: Dana, 14 years older; Janet, 7 years older; and Jim, a year younger.

It was rumored in the late 1930s that there were German submarines off the coast of Boston and further north due to sightings from the top of Blue Hill. Dad put together a mounted patrol as we and an uncle had horses and family riders available to search wooded areas. We found nothing but felt very patriotic.

I went to Smith College in 1941 and spent the four war years there. On Sunday, December 7, 1941, the weekend of the Charity Ball, my Princeton date and I returned from a picnic to learn that the Japanese had attacked Pearl Harbor. Our lives and those of our countrymen would never be the same. President Roosevelt declared war on Japan. On December 11, he also declared war on both Germany and Italy.

Many men, both young and middle aged, enlisted. A draft was instigated. A number of commodities were rationed: gasoline, meat, butter, cheese, food, cigarettes, tobacco, etc. Even salaries and prices were "frozen." We took buses and trains when we could.

During those four years, young friends or family members whom we knew or loved were killed or pronounced missing. It was a very tense and often sad time. Servicemen overseas sent V-mails to their families and sweethearts. A German student and friend of mine was considered an alien, allowed to stay but periodically had to report to a government agent.

Students actively participated in dorm jobs: front door bell duty, sorting mail, setting tables and helping both in the dining room and kitchen. Unheard of in peace time, the college set up a USO on the campus in the boathouse on Paradise Pond. Westover Field, an airbase, was not far from Northampton. We were allowed to become hostesses on Saturday night, with a rule of no fraternizing the next day. It was a rule that was not always observed. The pilots often flew their planes low over the roof of the gym where students sunbathed.

The WAVES arrived with Mrs. Horton, head of the WAVES (whom I knew later when she was President of Wellesley College). Sometimes it became risky walking or running to class if they were marching around the campus.

My brother Jim, who had become a paratrooper (he was eventually deployed overseas), came to visit in his spiffy uniform. I was so proud of him.

I joined a small singing group, the Octavians. We went to a couple of nearby Army hospitals and sang popular songs to the wounded soldiers. It was a joy to see them smile.

Summers we spent volunteering on farms, in hospitals, or anywhere we could be useful to the war effort. My first job was at the Crippled Children's Hospital in Canton (I rode my bike). In the following summers I took a train to Boston to the Massachusetts General Hospital, where I first assisted the Head of Nursing (a desk job), and later worked at the Allergy Clinic where I was the only one who sneezed. I also volunteered evenings at a Boston USO.

My mother, head of the Nursing Association, organized a bandage rolling group. My dad helped in the manufacturing of soldiers' uniforms.

Senior year I became engaged to Bill in a whirlwind trip to New York City. I recall his mother's diamond ring, flowers, champagne, many hugs and kisses, then off he went to New Jersey on his way to being shipped overseas for the next two years.

On the home front, those old and young, despite the deprivations (mostly minor) and heartache found meaningful, even humorous experiences in our support of one another, those we loved at home and overseas and in our country.

A native of Canton, Mass., Bailey graduated from Smith College. After working in advertising in Boston for several years, she worked at Cornell University in financial aid. Married to William C. Arthur Jr., she is the mother of four children and served as volunteer for several community organizations in Worcester, Mass.

Memories

Marcie Blauner

I was thirteen when the war began in 1941. My whole school was called to assembly to listen to Roosevelt's speech declaring war. I was not old enough to be really concerned and just young enough to be excited.

My brother was a freshman at Columbia. Most of his class left in 1943 to go to war. He was wounded in the Battle of the Bulge. I was concerned and returned from boarding school to console my parents. Their immediate reaction was one of relief—at least he was no longer in danger. He underwent many operations and was finally discharged from the Army. We had a Service Star hanging in our window.

I have many memories of that time: tin cans were flattened and recycled; there was no sugar; ration books; blackout curtains; no more silk stockings worn to dancing class—bobby socks only. My father was an air-raid warden and we had to have special permission from the Coast Guard to go out on the Long Island Sound in a boat. The mailman always rang the doorbell when we got a letter from my brother.

When Roosevelt died, I mourned with the nation. He was the only President I had ever known.

Marcie was born in New York City and grew up in nearby New Rochelle. She graduated from Smith College and was married to her late husband Justin, with whom she had three children.

My Friend Nobie

Mileva Brown

As an eight-year-old in Oakland, Calif., in 1941 I did not read newspapers or have television. All I knew was that Pearl Harbor had been attacked by Japanese airplanes and I expected those dreadful Zero airplanes to fly over quiet Holly Street at any moment.

Thankfully, my parents kept calm and protected me from the real world. I can recall the air raid drills and how we had to cover the windows with new blackout shades, white on the inside and dark on the outside. Since both our house and our school were relatively close to two training bases, one Army and one Navy, we were able to view many airplanes zooming overhead. For a child this was very exciting. We knew where they came from but had no idea where they were going. I remember especially the P38 with a kind of double tail. We learned the most from the Saturday afternoon movie newsreels. It was kind of scary.

For me, war meant rationing of nearly everything, food, gasoline, tires, and more. My mother served on the local ration board. In an effort to supplement our meat supply, my parents decided to raise chickens. Our home was in a suburb apparently with no restrictions regarding chickens. Each February for three or four years, my parents would go to a hatchery and purchase 80 baby chicks, 40 Rhode Island Reds and 40 Plymouth Rocks.

Dad built an elaborate brooder under a porch. Mom bought a book on how to raise chickens. According to the book, the feet of the chickens had to be kept clean. That was my job, to pick up each chick and clean their toenails. Then Dad built an area behind the garage with a ladder for the hens to climb and roost. It was beautiful. If a chicken didn't climb readily, I helped them.

As you can imagine we had a lot of eggs. Dad got tired of collecting them so he built a place inside so that the hens could lay their eggs in these nice cubicles and we could just go into the garage and pick them up. What to do with all those eggs? Angel food and sponge cake were staples for dessert. Since my mother was raised in a country setting, she was very talented at killing the chickens. She simply wrung their necks. Then it was my job to help remove the feathers. And, the neighbors were well supplied with eggs. I think this helped compensate for the noise of the crowing roosters.

Collecting newspapers and tin cans for recycling was exciting for me. We took newspapers to our elementary school classroom. Every week our principal, Mr. Brenner, would choose a student to follow him from room to room to measure the height of the paper piles. Periodically, the classroom with the most collected paper would receive a special prize or privilege. We also collected the tin foil wrappers from chewing gum to press into balls. Much later, I learned that these balls of foil were somehow used in the deflection of enemy radar.

I remember Nobuko Yoshida, a Japanese-American who was one of my best friends. Her family operated a large garden nursery, specializing in roses, near our school. In 1942, when the Japanese-Americans were whisked away to internment camps at Tule Lake, Calif., near the Oregon border, nobody explained to us what was happening.

In retrospect, it still amazes me that nobody at home or at school talked about what happened to the Yoshidas. The sign on the gate of their business simply said "closed for the duration." I never considered Nobie to be one of the "bad Japanese" who attacked our country. The Yoshidas were the only Japanese family that we knew.

Nobie rejoined our class for our senior year of high school, but somehow we never discussed her family's internment. We now know more details of the Japanese internment camps which are now considered an injustice but at that time were believed to be a necessary precaution.

A native of Oakland, Calif., Mileva graduated from the University of California, Berkeley and worked as a medical librarian. She and her husband Christopher had two children. She has worked as a hospital volunteer in Peterborough and serves on many committees at RiverMead.

Navy Corpsman in Training

George F. Cahill Jr., M.D.

In June, 1945, I left Yale after three terms to join the Navy. I was sent to Naval Training Station, Sampson, N.Y., for ten weeks of basic training at boot camp. In August I left on a ten-day train trip to San Diego, where I started training to be a Navy Corpsman, from which I graduated first in my class. My next station was at Oak Knoll Naval Hospital in Oakland, CA. and I was preparing to be with a Marine unit in the invasion of Japan. However, the atomic bomb ended that possibility.

For the next year, I stayed at Oak Knoll as Pharmacist Mate third class and Head Corpsman of the Senior Ward office. I also played on the basketball and baseball teams and edited the hospital newspaper, *The Sentinel*.

I passed the exam to be promoted to Pharmacist Mate second class, but the Navy would not promote me unless I enlisted for four more years. I declined and was discharged in February 1947 and returned to Yale and graduated in 1949. From there I went to Columbia for my M.D., which I received with top honors, and then to Peter Bent Brigham Hospital in Boston to begin my medical career.

A native of New York City, George graduated from Hotchkiss Academy, Yale and Columbia earning his medical degree and spending his career in academic medical research and teaching, including four years at Columbia, 36 yrears at Harvard Medical School and eight years at Dartmouth. He and his late wife Sally had six children.

A Surgeon is Born

Robert A. Chase, M.D.

On December 7, 1941, "The Day of Infamy" at Pearl Harbor, I was a pre-medical student at the University of New Hampshire. Because of the need for physicians we pre-meds were put on an accelerated schedule. I was accepted at Yale University School of Medicine in 1943. I was then taken into the Navy as an apprentice seaman first class and supported during medical school. About fifty percent of the male members of my medical school class were on active duty—half in the Army and half in the Navy—during the four-year medical school curriculum which we completed in three calendar years.

After graduation we spent a short time on regular active duty after which we were surveyed out and discharged. I then started residency training in surgery at Yale and to gain financial support I enlisted into the regular Army as a First Lieutenant on a year-for-year payback arrangement.

When the Korean War started I was called out of residency to serve as Chief Surgeon at Fort Monmouth, N.J., the Signal Corps headquarters. After serving a year or so there the Surgeon General's office offered me a transfer to Valley Forge Army General Hospital in Phoenixville, Pa. This hospital had served as a plastic surgery and hand-surgery center during WWII and it was one of only two hand-surgery center hospitals during the Korean War.

I accepted this opportunity with a request to be assigned to the Hand Center and eventually I became head of the Center. We had a running census of more than 200 hand- and upper-limb-injury patients during my stay there.

I worked with Dr. Erie Peacock and with our consultant Dr. J. William Littler, who commuted from New York every two weeks to operate and consult with us. Littler was, in my view, the greatest hand surgeon in the world and Peacock was the best of his many students. We researched new procedures and techniques and had tremendous experience with upper-limb problems. We were also influenced greatly by the records and models left by the great plastic surgeons who worked at Valley Forge during WWII.

The experience at Valley Forge had a determining effect on my career in surgery. I was promoted to Captain and as the Korean War subsided I was ordered back into the Yale Surgery program to finish residency training and, bless the Army, they let me stay an extra year upon my being chosen chief resident surgeon at Yale in 1954.

Upon leaving Yale my family (My wife Ann and three children) and I continued my active duty in Italy. I was Chief of Surgery at the Station Hospital in Livorno, Italy where I was responsible for all surgery including specialties such as Orthopedics, Neurosurgery, Urology, Otolaryngology, etc.

In addition I was responsible personally for all obstetrics and gynecology. When I arrived I found that there were thirty women at term in my territory and many challenging surgical cases. Our hospital served more than 200-300 servicemen and their families from all over Italy. I truly loved the experience and the family very much enjoyed living in northern Italy at that time.

In fact the experience was so interesting that I petitioned the surgeon general's office to extend our stay for an extra year which they were delighted to do. They later tried to persuade me to stay in the regular army to retirement but I already had plans to respond to an invitation to return to Yale as a faculty member in the department of surgery. Since I had gained more and more experience in reconstructive surgery and had great enthusiasm for it I asked the chairman of surgery at Yale to be allowed two years to get proper credentials in Reconstructive and Plastic surgery before returning to Yale. This I did as a fellow in Plastic Surgery at the University of Pittsburgh before returning to Yale to develop its first plastic surgery division. After several years on the faculty at Yale I was promoted to Associate Professor of surgery. I was then offered the great opportunity to become Professor and Chairman for all of Surgery at Stanford University in California.

In summary my 12 years in the Navy and Army had an enormous influence on my career. I had the opportunity to care for many service people with wartime injuries as well as a broad array of surgical and obstetrical problems. I shall be forever grateful to the US services for this. I could not have afforded the medical and surgical education and training without the financial support received from the services during those early years.

Born and raised in Keene, N.H., Robert and his wife Ann have three children, nine grandchildren and nine great grandchildren.

SPIES IN CONNECTICUT

Barbara Clark

I lived in Pine Orchard, Conn., a small community on Long Island Sound. During World War II we all did our part for the war effort as best we could. My mother spotted airplanes for defense and kept our household running with the use of food ration stamps. We walked everywhere to save driving cars which were used only in emergencies as gas was rationed.

At the age of 12 my duties were limited to rolling bandages, knitting hats for servicemen, collecting tin cans for the war effort, and my major job at home was to squeeze a plastic bag until the gelatin pill broke and turned the oleo ingredients to yellow.

Many times our family entertained British sailors and children who were sent to the states for safe keeping from the bombing in England.

One very important job was to draw our dark shades at night to "black out" the lights in our homes. There was a concern that Nazis submarines could come down the Sound from New London, Conn., to drop off Nazis spies. The subs could get into New London under the ships going through the nets. We all thought this to be farfetched until we heard that spies had indeed come ashore and been captured in the next town.

We always took our jobs seriously and felt we were helping on the road to victory.

Born in New Rochelle, N.Y., Barbara grew up in Pine Orchard, Conn. She graduated from Lesley University in Cambridge, Mass. and worked as an elementary school teacher and tutor. She spent many years in community service. She and her husband, Thomas "Cap" Clark, had three sons.

LIFE AT THE NORFOLK NAVAL BASE

JUDITH E. COLLIER

It was December 7th, 1941. We lived in quarters at the Norfolk Naval Base in Norfolk Va. My father, George Chase Emery, an architect, had joined the Navy at the suggestion of a navy friend in Denver. In August 1941, my mother and father, my 10-year-old brother and the 12-year-old me had moved from Denver to Virginia. My father had been commissioned as a lieutenant in the Civil Engineering Corps and as an officer we could live in quarters on the Naval Base.

George Chase Emery

    I shall always remember that Sunday. At 3 o'clock in the afternoon we had been listening to a New York Philharmonic Symphony concert and suddenly the music was interrupted. A news announcer came on to tell us that Pearl Harbor has been attacked and very shortly war was declared. We were stunned and wondered what it meant. For us living on the base it meant dark shades on every window in the house, the men having access to guns, constant announcements on the radio about the status of the war, gas rationing, food rationing, tighter security going in and out of the gates of the base and anxiety about the unknowns of war. It meant sadness and grief as news came of sons of friends dying and missing in action.

    My father was working very hard and we did not see much of him those days. He was constantly involved in the effects the war was having on the military. My mother joined other women and made bandages and other necessary items for the men overseas but my brother and I lived a pretty normal school life. We attended the Norfolk public schools so we were bused from the base to and from school. At that point I was more disturbed when riding on the street car from the base into town and seeing racial prejudice. The colored people were obliged to sit in the back of the street cars: I had never seen that before. And yet they served in the Navy for our country. I remember my father coming home one afternoon happily telling us that the first "colored man" had graduated from Annapolis and was to be stationed at the Norfolk Naval Base.

Because my father served in the Civil Engineering Corps and not the ship serving line, the family lived together most of the war. After three years in Norfolk my father was transferred to the Mechanicsburg Supply Base in Pennsylvania where he was in charge of supply forces and the welfare of the base. Occasionally he would do some architectural work for the base. We lived nearby in private housing in Camp Hill, Pa., for three years.

In my senior year in high school, 1946-47, my father was sent to Guam, but the families could not go. It was hard for my mother, for the next year I went off to college and my brother went off to private school and she was left alone. So we were definitely affected by the war, not on the battlefield but in many other ways.

My father served in the Navy for 20 years having duty in the Boston Naval Shipyard, the Pentagon in Washington DC, Quonset Point in Rhode Island, Paris, France and Long Beach, Calif. He was retired as a Captain, beloved and outstanding leader and lived five more years in retirement in Chatham, Mass.

A native of Lincoln, Mass., Judith attended Oberlin College and worked as a teacher before raising her family of five children with her husband, Robert G. Millican D.M.D. She also volunteered for numerous school, civic and community organizations.

Dear Dad

Warner B. Cornwall

I have your letter and I will try to clear up some of the difficulties you speak of. Things have been rather twisted up and at times I have not understood them myself. Briefly, this is what happened:

1) I was sworn into the Army Aug. 4

2) I was sent to the Reception Center at Ft. Devens Aug. 18

3) I was assigned to the technical division of the Air Force

4) I was shipped to the Air Force Replacement Training Center at Miami Beach. Went through 18-day basic training there.

5) I was classified as a machinist and was to be sent to a special school for further training. However, as I am 1-B ("limited service") due to my eyes, I am not allowed to go to machinist school and have been reclassified as "permanent party." That meant I was to be permanently stationed here at Miami Beach.

6) I was then shipped to the Officer Candidate School for general duty. This Air Force Officers Candidate School might well be 1,000 miles away from the Replacement Training Center, but as it happens is only a few miles up the beach.

I am attached to Squadron 649 whose job it is to work in the kitchens, dining rooms and hotels which make up the O.C.S. I work in the kitchen washing dishes every other day from 5 in the morning until 7 at night. On the day between I work on general detail around the hotels. Yesterday we put on hurricane shutters and another day I unloaded a supply truck, etc.

Usually manage to get in for a swim two or three times a week in the late afternoon. Live in the new Traymore Hotel at about 24th and Collins. Right on the water, and is really quite nice.

My present hope and plan is this: Of all the Officer Candidate Schools there is one called the Army Administrative which is primarily for "limited service" men. This is the only OCS in the Air

Force that I am qualified for. After Oct. 4th, when I shall have been in the Army for two months, I shall make application to go to this school. I would then have to wait until after Nov. 4 before I could be accepted. It is necessary to be in the Army three months before actually going to any OCS.

My Squadron Commander, Captain Fitzpatrick, has already assured me of his recommendation. Any others that I can submit would be helpful. I will write you about that when the time comes. In the meantime I will continue to do whatever comes up here. That is all I can do. It would be great if Nancy could come down now while I am waiting. The OCS is a 3-month course and it might well be that I stayed here for that time.

I hope this has cleared things up somewhat. Please do not take it as being definite for the whole situation may change within a week. It is impossible to forecast anything in the Army.
Love, Warner

Born in Melrose, Mass., Warner grew up in Ashburnham, Mass., and attended Tabor Academy. He worked in sales and marketing with the Heywood Wakefield Co. in Gardner, Mass., and later joined with his second wife, Francis, at Image Productions, a television production firm in New Canaan and Norwalk, Conn. He had three step children. Mr. Cornwall, 91, died in August 2011.

Snapshots of War

Julie Crocker, M.D.

I was 14 in Westchester, N.Y., in 1941. Many of my memories are snapshots of how the war affected my family life. I remember gas rationing curtailing auto travel, which meant that I first lived at school during the week and then full time. Sugar rationing demanded creativity in cooking. I argued with my sister to see who got to massage the yellow color pellet into oleomargarine, which was a substitute for butter rations. I drove a two-cylinder yellow Crosley that had a "dip stick" as a gasoline gauge and I frequently would run out of gas! I also saved the bits of tin foil (often from cigarette packs) and made them into large balls for recycling.

Kes Schoepf

It was a time of oversized clothes and I proudly wore the tweed jacket of my 6'4" brother, to the envy of many schoolmates. Kes could not get into the Army Air Corps because he did not have a high school diploma. He was a superb athlete but had trouble with his academic work. From a review of his letters home, we now know that he was (at least) dyslectic. He was able to get a document from the Taft School stating that he had completed 12 years of schooling. He also had a pilot's license. On this basis the Canadian Air Force accepted him. It was 1941 when he transferred to the U.S. Army Air Corps as a 1st Lieutenant. He was killed in August 1943, over the Gulf of Salerno, near Naples, Italy, while on a reconnaissance mission as an observer. I happened to be home and answered the telephone when the call came from the War Department that he was missing in action. I remember that the house was very quiet afterwards. He was the only son and the last with the family surname.

When I was a freshman at Vassar in 1944, I found myself in queues to buy rationed cigarettes for my friends. Unfortunately, I decided to see what this was about and became addicted for 20 years.

When my husband, Gus, graduated from Harvard, he could not decide whether to become a music critic or a physician. He spent a year selling music and block flutes, as well as writing concert reviews in New York City. Fortunately for his patients, he decided on medicine and graduated from Tufts Medical School in October of 1944. While he was in medical school he joined the A.S.T.P. (Army Specialized Training Program), which covered his medical tuition and obligated him for service in the armed forces. His internship was at the Boston City Hospital, after which he trained at Carlisle Barracks, Pa., and Fort Devens, Mass. and was inducted into the U.S. Army Medical Corps.

Despite the fact that he wanted to become an internist, he was posted to a Victory ship out of Bremerhaven, Germany, carrying war brides back to the USA. He told some wonderful stories. The brides were supposed to be not more than six months pregnant, but one delivered a full-term child on the deck before they left harbor. The thought that it might be a decidedly premature infant caused a great deal of chaos. One of the nurses made several trips and they never suspected that she was pregnant. Those aprons, you know!

The brides were told to bring enough formula for the babies to last the voyage, so they lugged trunks of formula on board. The only problem was that the ship had only two tiny kitchens for hundreds of infants. And, there was no refrigeration for the bottles. And, each mother had a different recipe/product. And, the other doctor on board was more interested in surgery. So Gus and his colleague had to figure out some sort of dietary program for all the babies as a compromise. They interviewed the women to find out how much material went into a bottle. One bride's response was: "Oh, two scoops and a dash."

Gus was discharged in 1947, served a residency at the Boston City Hospital in 1948-9, and a research fellowship in cardiology with Dr. Samuel Levine at the Peter Bent Brigham 1950-2. We became engaged in the summer of 1952 and planned a June wedding in Dublin, when I would graduate from medical school. Unfortunately, his uncle, as head of the doctors' procurement program in Boston, informed him that he was to be re-drafted for the Korean conflict because he was six days short of service in WWII. We were married in December. Luckily, he was drafted into the USAF this time and served as chief of medicine at Chicopee Air Force Base in Massachusetts for a short time before they changed this law.

Born in Detroit, Julie grew up in Scarsdale, N.Y. and graduated from Vassar College, earned a Masters in zoology at Columbia and her M.D. from the Columbia College of Physicians and Surgeons. She worked as an anesthesiologist. With her late husband Augustus T. Crocker M.D., she had three children.

The Inverted Spin

James Faller

It was midwinter in the mid-forties when I arrived at Naval Air Station Glenview, one of the Navy's several primary flight-training bases, just north of Chicago. I had just finished pre-flight training at the University of Iowa in Iowa City.

The basic training airplane at that time was a Stearman canvas-covered biplane with two open cockpits, the front one for the instructor and the rear one for the student. Communication between the two was through a tube connected to the student's ears in his helmet. Return talk was impossible, so a shake of the student's head, yes or no, was the reply to the questions of the instructor. He could see the student in a small rear-view mirror mounted under the top wing.

The flight uniform in cold weather consisted of a heavy flight suit and large fleece-lined boots, gloves, and helmet. Our first flight was a familiarization mission, to show the student the traffic patterns leaving and entering the base, and the several outlying fields where takeoffs and landings were practiced.

After my young instructor finished with all this, he asked whether I had ever done an inverted spin. After I shook my head no, he said he would begin one, and I should recover when he told me to. Even an inexperienced pilot like me knew how to do that: Lower the plane's nose to regain air speed. What I hadn't experienced before was the pressure on the seatbelt in an inverted stalled airplane. He did a half loop, stalled the upside-down plane, and looked in the rear-view mirror at the rapidly disappearing body of the student behind him. I had reached for something to hang on to, and my large sleeve had hooked on to my seatbelt and unlatched it. Luckily my heavy boots had caught under the instrument panel. He quickly recovered and I plopped back into my seat. He thought this was quite funny, but I think both of us realized what would have happened if I had parachuted into some friendly farmer's frozen field and how he would have explained to his superiors his return to base with an empty rear seat.

I had a lot of experiences after graduating from Pensacola and becoming a dive-bomber pilot and a member of an air group with many flights from an aircraft carrier, yet that first training flight remains one of my most unforgettable.

The era of my Navy flying was before jet aircraft, ship-based rescue helicopters, and modern day super-carriers powered by nuclear engines, and with angled decks that allow a landing pilot to take off again in the event his trailing tailhook fails to catch one of the several arresting cables. The landing signal officer with his two waving paddles has disappeared, replaced with something more suitable for today's high speed airplanes. These modern ships separate berthing facilities for male and female sailors, something unheard of in earlier times.

My almost ten years in the service was equally split between active duty and, later, the organized flying reserve. The latter was where I flew other types of carrier aircraft - fighters and torpedo planes.

After resigning from the Navy, I have owned two civilian single-engine planes, and have amassed many additional flying hours, so my log books total over two thousand. But my flying days are over. Without a current medical certificate my former commercial instrument rated license is no longer valid.

A native of Buffalo, N.Y., James attended Cornell University and worked as a manufacturers' representative in engineering sales. He and his wife, the late Suzanne Faller, had four children.

WHEN THE WAR BONDS PAID OFF

SHARON H. GOLDSMITH

In the summer of 1941 my young parents moved their family from the wheat lands of rural eastern Oregon to the big city of Portland, Ore., where my father had a job at the First National Bank of Portland. Our new home on N.E. 51st Street was small and cozy but had a big backyard. My first five years of education had been in a progressive school with only twenty five children in grades 1-12. By the fourth grade I had already read all of the high school material. We had wonderful teachers and freedom to look into anything we were interested in.

I loved my new "experimental" school because there were lots of great kids. At the beginning of my first year a few of us were given the opportunity to visit the Kaiser Shipyards where Russian merchant marine ships came in to be re-outfitted. Russian families travelled on those ships and we got to play and be with the Russian children who wanted to practice their English with us.

Then came December 7, 1941. I remember listening to President Roosevelt speak to the nation on the big radio at the table in our tiny dining room with the upright piano at the end of the room. Portland immediately instituted blackouts with all windows covered at night. As a child I had the sense of everybody working together and I felt safe and protected. My mother began taking care of a sweet and beautiful two year old child. Her father was in the service and her mother had moved from the south to come work as a "Rosie the Riveter" at the Kaiser Shipyards which were in full production of war ships. The little girl spent weekdays with us and her mother, still wearing her heavy welding clothing, would pick her up on Friday evenings.

Mother and Dad did their part by taking on extra war jobs two nights a week at a small munitions factory. My sister Derrie and I contributed to the war effort by collecting aluminum from our neighbors. We would go from house to house asking for contributions. Aluminum was a challenge for me to pronounce so I would practice saying, "Do you have any extra aluminum?"

In the summer of 1942 my father relieved rural bank managers so they could have a summer vacation. The rest of us stayed with Grandma Akers, and when he was finished, went on our family camping and fishing vacation. We ended the summer with my sister and me spending two weeks at Girl Scout Camp.

A Mrs. Baisley had a tiny "drugstore" near our home. Dad had spoken to her about me and I was offered a job making 25 cents an hour working Saturday and Sundays. I was only 12. I'm told I was one of the youngest persons to receive a Social Security number in Portland. Mrs. Baisley lived at the store. She had a small cot at the back and a nasty Pekinese dog whom I never liked. I made money orders and bank deposits and ran the little ice cream counter. I remember when a box of Hershey Bars arrived, Mrs. Baisley would ration them out to her best customers.

Dad and I discussed what I would do with my salary and it was decided I would take half of my earnings and buy eight Savings Bond stamps at school each Monday morning. I was the biggest purchaser of stamps at school and I felt proud as I stuck each stamp into my book. At the end of nine weeks I had $18 worth of stamps. My family would all chip in the last 75 cents to fill up my book. After that we would all have a little celebration. At the end of the school year I had completed four and a half twenty-five-dollar books.

On June 5, 1944, I was graduating from 8th grade. Grandma Akers came down from Wasco to be there. She had brought me a beautiful ring with my birthstone in it. I was so excited about this special present and while we were looking at it in our tiny dining room, the phone rang. After my parents got off the phone they said they would be leaving immediately with Grandma for San Francisco. Uncle Wayne, my mother's oldest brother, was a major in the Army and the head administrator at the Letterman Army Hospital in San Francisco, overseeing the admissions of all the incoming soldiers who had been transported from the Pacific Theater. When my parents arrived in San Francisco, the chaplain explained that the son of Uncle Wayne's best friend had arrived badly wounded. My uncle had gone into his office and killed himself with his service revolver.

About a month later we went as usual to Grandma's while dad relieved the bank managers for their vacations. The day after we arrived Grandma died peacefully in her sleep. Grandma left me her little upright piano which was sold for $25 and a savings bond was purchased bringing my bond total to 12.

Mom and Dad were both the youngest children of their large families. Although many of their nephews fought in Europe, they all came home safely, so Grandma and Uncle Wayne were the only casualties of WW II in our family.

Traditionally Dad would take his vacation the first two weeks of August and our family would go camping and fishing in the beautiful woods of Oregon. That year it was such a comfort for all of us to be together and enjoy the serenity and power of nature which Grandma had always loved as well. My sister and I would then spend the last two weeks at Girl Scout Camp which was totally different with fun camp songs and rowdy young girls.

My first year of high school was very difficult. The war news was terrible from Europe and the South Pacific. I felt I was just plodding along walking an hour to school each way every day. As I look back, those long walks were good for me as I enjoyed nature and the exercise cleared my head. At that time, my mother began visiting her sister in Los Angeles. In 1945 we didn't go on our usual family camping trip in August. Mom and Dad were both in L.A. where my dad was looking for a job. My brother was with Aunt Pearl and my sister and I were back home getting ready for Girl Scout Camp when, on August 6th, the atomic bomb was dropped on Hiroshima and three days later on Nagasaki. Things began to fall into place. Dad was offered a job with Bank of America in L.A., and it seemed the end of the war was coming soon. Just as we were headed to camp, VJ Day came and everyone at the Girl Scout Camp was so light hearted and happy that year. When Dad picked us up from camp we were so thrilled about the move that we sang camp songs all the way to L.A. Aunt Ruth became my musical mentor and most special aunt.

Aunt Ruth found us a house to rent in Burbank in exchange for taking care of the owner's little girl. We moved into our new home about three days before school started. I had a 45-minute walk to Burbank High School. There was a new Thrifty Drugstore being built at the end of our street. I went up and applied for a weekend job. I got the job even though I was a year too young. Every time the union person came to the store, I would go upstairs to the bathroom until he left. I was making $1 an hour!!! That $1 an hour was still in force in 1950 when I had a weekend job at a radio/TV station.

I was married in 1950, and had my first child in 1952. In July 1954 my parents came from Burbank to celebrate Ellen's second birthday. My parents always made birthdays special and this was no exception. Birthdays always made them feel like children again themselves. Mother always made the cake and the decorations were wonderful and fun.

I had totally forgotten about things like war bonds and so when my father presented me with $300 cash I was dumbfounded. My parents had been able to cash in my bond books. My Grandmother's piano money had put me over the top to reach $300 and now those bonds had just matured! The timing was perfect. We needed a car! We had just purchased our first little home in the valley, and we were getting packed up for our move. A couple of days later Dad came back and he and I went to a used car dealership. We immediately found the perfect car for exactly $300. This was the first and only time I was able to purchase an automobile for the exact amount I needed or wanted to spend.

Sharon was born in The Dalles, Ore., but moved with her family to Southern California right after World War II. There she attended Los Angeles City College and UCLA. After singing with the Los Angeles Civic Light Opera, she married composer Jerry Goldsmith, who wrote and conducted the scores for many significant WW II films, including Von Ryan's Express, Patton, Tora, Tora, Tora *and* MacArthur. *Together they had four children. Sharon returned to UCLA in 1973 where she received a certification in psychiatric social work.*

Uncle Bob Missing in Action

Molly Goodnow

I was five when Pearl Harbor was attacked. I had no idea what had happened but had a distinct feeling that the world around me had suddenly hushed. Something dreadful had happened. Something very scary.

The war, as with most other Americans, deeply affected our immediate family. My mother was the eldest of five siblings and not as directly involved because my father was a few months over the draft age but also because he was running a foundry whose products were important to the war effort. It was not so easy with her other four brothers and sisters.

My Aunt Grace married her newly graduated West Point husband. Then off he was to the Pacific as a fresh second Lieutenant in the newly formed Army Air Corps. During a few months at this time, Aunt Gay took me to Sanibel Island, Fla., where my grandmother lived. Every night before a chapter of Uncle Wiggley's tales was read to me, we sang the newly composed Army Air Corps song. Uncle Symmie returned from the war with scars and with malaria. Both of these seemed to subdue him, taking away much of his beloved zest and wit.

Another aunt, Elinor, married her sweetheart before their originally planned wedding because he also was called to the war in the Pacific. While flying a mission his plane was hit and disabled by enemy fire. He ordered his men to bail out and held the plane as steady as possible for them to evacuate. His crew was saved but Uncle Bob was declared Missing in Action. Aunt Ellie came to wait for a call from the Air Force at my parents' home in Erie, Pa. Despite my youth, I could sense her anguish. My parents asked that none of our friends telephone unless very necessary. A Missing in Action cardboard notice was placed in a window beside the front door. No call came for Aunt Ellie, good or bad.

Two other uncles were also pilots, one protecting the west coast of the US and the other flying bombing missions in Europe and later flying the dreaded Berlin Air Lift corridor. Neither of them wished to talk about the war, not immediately after victory or even years later.

Personally, every night I slept as far away as possible from a window, somehow thinking this would better protect me from enemy bombs that the Air Raid Warden warned may be coming. At school I hated those dratted Air Raid drills where we huddled under our desks until the All Clear sounded. One day, our principal announced over the loud speaker system that we hurry outside to see the first jet airplane fly across the sky. It, frankly, didn't seem very interesting to me ... until the air was split in half by the sonic boom.

I remember the Christmas my mother stood in line for over two hours to get me a real rubber doll, one that even wet. Most rubber was reserved for the war effort. I can still picture my Aunt Ellie stitching clothes for my doll and waiting for the phone to ring.

We kids tried to help by gathering milkweed pods, the innards of which were used for making life vests buoyant. I can still picture my wet wool snow suit, covered with the milkweed fuzz, hanging close to the furnace in hopes of drying before school the next day. Remember saving tin cans? After using the contents, we opened the closed end of the can, inserted the two covers within the can, then flattened it by jumping on it. How about stirring a yellow dye into some kind of lard-type substance to help pretend it was butter? One year my mother made grape jelly. Having a surplus of brown sugar rationing coupons, she substituted that for white cane sugar. Not once since that disaster have I had grape jam, jelly or preserves.

A native of Erie, Pa., Molly attended the Grier School and Duke University. She worked for the Central Intelligence Agency in Washington D.C., and for Army Counter-Intelligence in Stuttgart, Germany. She also served as a Trustee of the Keene Public Library for more than 23 years. She and her husband Sym have two children.

ENGINEERING AND EXPEDITING

POLLY GOTTSCHALK

In 1943, the U.S. Army Corps of Engineers came to Taunton, Mass., to participate in the building of Camp Myles Standish, a staging area for troops going overseas. I was secretary to a lieutenant in the Corps during that time.

When it was completed, the engineers left and I was transferred to their Providence office in the Industrial Trust building. There I was secretary to a captain and was subsequently promoted to be an "expediter" checking up, by phone, on companies in southern New England who were making supplies for the Army to make sure they delivered them in a timely fashion.

I worked there until the end of the war.

Polly is a native of Brockton, Mass., and a graduate of Simmons College. With her husband, Nathan, she had two children and volunteered in the PTA, and for the Albany and Pioneer Valley Symphony Orchestras.

The Little Nite Club

Susanne Holcombe

Bob was stationed at Camp Lee in Virginia while doing his Army basic training as an auto mechanic. Our address was c/o The Little Nite Club, Petersburg, Va. My mother was first shocked and then amused.

My two children and I lived in an apartment next to The Little Nite Club. It was a converted Cadillac showroom which had been divided into two apartments with a bathroom in between which we shared with Sergeant Smigo and his family. This presented a priority problem when the two men were in residence. The sergeant had the right of way, and in fact the sergeant would not even communicate with the private.

The laundry set-up was more troublesome. Mrs. Smigo and I took turns washing the diapers in the bathtub. We hung them on a clothes line strung on a pulley out behind the building but we had to time it just right: If the local steam train came along, the washing would be covered with soot and the process would have to be repeated.

Two elderly men who ran The Little Nite Club lived below us. They loved the children and kept us safe for the duration of our stay, until the end of basic training.

A native of Cambridge, Mass., Bob Holcombe received his B.A. from Harvard College and his M.B.A. at the Harvard School of Business. He spent his career in sales in the container shipping industry. He served on his town's Budget Committee, supported the Visiting Nurse Association and was president of his ski and tennis clubs. He and his wife Susanne had three children.

SOUTH MEETS NORTH

CHRISTINE S. KELLY

Lt. jg Ed Kelly

In 1943 I was leading a Southern life in Mobile, Ala. One day a friend called and asked me if I would like to have a blind date. I didn't like the idea, but said I would join her.

Lieutenant jg Ed Kelly, dressed in his Navy Air Corps uniform, charming and handsome, appeared at my door to pick me up. We went off to a restaurant and started the evening drinking French 75s, a brandy concoction which they brought with them with all the ingredients mixed. We had a wonderful time drinking the French 75s and dancing. He knocked me off my feet!

I had seen Ed before at the Officer's Club when I was dating his commanding officer. "We have to get rid of him," Ed said. When he brought me home he tried to kiss me. I gave him a kiss on the cheek. My mother was waiting anxiously for me. "Oh Chris, isn't he charming?" she said. I agreed with her but noted, "He has a Yankee accent and talks funny." My mother assured me that that was OK. The next morning flowers arrived. The dates continued. We married in May of 1944, even though my friends were dubious about my marrying a "damn Yankee."

We lived on the base where Ed was stationed until he was sent to Atlanta to be trained in transport planes. I was pregnant and had our baby just before he was sent to Honolulu, Hawaii. I returned to Mobile to live with my parents. When he finished his training, Ed flew to Guam with supplies and brought back wounded soldiers on his return trip.

When the war ended in 1945, our family of three moved to West Hartford where Ed returned to Trinity College to finish his degree.

A native of Mobile, Ala., Christine moved north with her husband, Edmond (left), who spent his career in the family paper mill in Fitchburg, Mass. She and Ed had four children. She volunteered for several Red Cross community services.

My Special Day

Augusta Foster Law, M.D.

It was 1946. VE Day had been declared in Europe on May 8, 1945, and VJ Day in Japan on September 2. While most in the world celebrated, I had a special reason later to be thankful, too.

My brother was being transferred from the Atlantic to the Pacific Theater: his last assignment. He had been at sea in the Atlantic, the Pacific and in Europe for several years, and now he would have a whole day of shore leave in Boston. He was going to spend that whole day with me.

My brother

Our family was close. There were four of us and we were great friends. We worked, we traveled, we played bridge, we had hobbies, and life was good.

Then, suddenly, Brother left college and enlisted. This separation was hard for my parents and me. We missed him greatly, but most of all, we were so afraid for his life. We knew that his ship was transporting aviation fuel in the Pacific and that just before he boarded it had shot down an attacking Japanese plane.

At that time, I was finishing medical school, my last assignment before graduation. My clinical clerkship was at one of the large state mental hospitals in Worcester, Mass. I was able to get most of the day off but first had to update some information on several patients placed in the most difficult of the back wards (which, fortunately, are no more).

I had planned for Brother to come with me as I finished up my patient progress reports. Since many of the students were seen in their Navy uniforms, I hoped that no one would notice that Brother's uniform was that of an engineer, and not that of a medical officer. Who would notice the difference? Anyway, having seen enemy planes and missiles overhead and witnessed the air raids in London, I felt Brother could accompany me as I finished my work.

The rest of the day was special for both of us. We went sightseeing around Boston. We visited and lunched with relatives. We met and dined with some of his new friends, then parted with the happy knowledge that his return to civilian life and college was in the near future.

The next day, the last of my assignment, I was called in by the medical personnel officer. He asked about my experiences at the hospital, and I was able to express appreciation and gratitude for all I had learned. He told me that the staff had appreciated my good work, but that I had committed a serious infraction by bringing my brother onto the wards with me; that he, a young engineer, had seen situations where only staff should be present. He told me that because of this I could receive only a passing grade, then he asked me my plans for the four months until graduation. I told him that I was headed back to med school to see about a job that would give me experience, room and board until that time. He invited me to stay at the hospital and continue what I was doing.

This day was a special one for both of us; one we always remembered. Brother returned to college then stayed in the Naval Reserves for twenty years. I was pleased to stay at the hospital.

Gus was born in Sargentville, Maine and graduated with degrees from the University of Maine, Tufts University School of Medicine, and the Harvard School of Public Health. She worked for a short time with her husband, Dr. Alexandre Law, in family practice in Milford, N.H. She also worked in Public Health for the state of New Hampshire for some 20 years.

Moving Around with the "FlyBoys"

Helen W. Livingston

Graduation from Concord Academy in June 1941 and matriculation at Sarah Lawrence the following September may have been highlights of my young life at the time, but they were soon overshadowed by the horror of December 7th of that year and the events that followed.

My agenda in early 1942 did not include thoughts of marriage but that too was changed by a handsome young Naval Air Force cadet. We became engaged and in December were married and settled in Hutchinson, Kan., where Tim, having earned his wings, was training midshipmen and where I became indoctrinated into "life with the flyboys." This was intended to be a six-month assignment but turned out to be a year-and-a-half tour of duty. That gave us time to help convert an old warehouse into an officer's club and, although Kansas was a "dry" state, we were able to orchestrate a few bi-wing booze runs to Kansas City, Mo.

After a three or four month "hitch" in Glenview, Ill., where Tim was still an instructor, we were transferred to the Naval Air Transport Service in Atlanta, Ga., where Tim learned to fly the DC-3s. With his parent's contribution of a 1939 Packard sedan, I drove to Atlanta to be with Tim. That was an easy trip except for a flat tire in Charlotte, N.C., which required an appearance before the Tire Board to get approval for a retread. Following a week in Atlanta we moved on to Roanoke, Va., for further training.

About that time I experienced an embarrassing incident. I was standing in a lunch line at a local cafeteria when I passed out. I was told that pregnancy could do that to you. In any event, I was carried through the kitchen to the waitress' resting room where I was revived and ministered to with care. When I was able to regain my mobility, I discovered that one of my loafers was missing. After a frustrating search throughout the facility the missing shoe was found nicely warmed in the mashed potato vat.

Mid summer 1944 we were sent to Florida. We lived in Miami Beach and then Hialeah. Tim was flying supplies to the Caribbean and Rio de Janeiro. On one night flight his engine developed a "cough and a sneeze," calling for an emergency landing. People on the ground could hear the unusual sounds and arranged lights to mark a landing strip. It turned out that mechanics had left an oil rag in a fuel line. A less dangerous but interesting flight was to Buenos Aires to pick up the crew of the Graf Spee after its surrender. It was during this period that our daughter Debbie was born - a much happier event.

The joys of V-J Day were marred by my having a gall-bladder attack. I was to fly with our three-month-old daughter back to be with my parents but was "bumped" in Jacksonville by other service personnel. Although Tim was headed for an assignment in California, he was able to get a leave and drove us non-stop to New York City leaving a trail of new-fashioned disposable diapers. The trip was fine but on arrival I had another attack which resulted in surgery. This was done by Dr. Allen O. Whipple who had just introduced a new procedure now known as the Whipple Method.

Casualties of the war have been well documented. Although not as dramatic but equally traumatizing and inadequately treated were some of the post-war psychological problems. Tim had been a vibrant and bright officer but became a walking collection of fears. He never flew again, could scarcely get into an elevator, and he drank much too much. The arrival of second daughter, Lisa, was a joy but not a solution. After ten years of marriage, we were divorced.

Years later I married Putnam Livingston with whom I had a third daughter, Martha. We were together more than thirty years until Put died at the end of eleven years of Alzheimer's disease. Twelve years went by, living then in Keene, N.H., before I married - for the third and final time - John Calhoun, who died here at RiverMead where we had lived happily since 2005.

Helen grew up in Weston, Mass. and graduated from Concord Academy and attended Sarah Lawrence College. In addition to raising her three children, she served on the boards of numerous non-profit organizations, including the Boston YWCA, the Henry Street Settlement in New York, the YWCA, the United Way in Summit, N.J. and Union County, N.J., Concord Academy, the Monadnock United Way, Monadnock Family Service and the Monadnock Alzheimer's Disease Association.

NO ORDINARY TIME

MARY ELIZABETH MCCLELLAN

(Excerpts from a Heritage Dinner Talk in York, Pa., on November 4, 1995)

What did I do on the home front between December 7, 1941, Pearl Harbor Day, and August 14, 1945, V-J Day? I was 18 years old when it started and 21 years old when it ended, and it was "No Ordinary Time."

In some ways, I did what I would have done in peace time: went to college, fell in and out of love, played bridge and tennis, hung out at the poolside of the country club, volunteered for Community Service with the Visiting Nurse Association, and dreamed of being a wife and mother.

But there was a difference. Fear and danger were abroad in the land, and everything was heightened: good guys vs. bad guys. It was no ordinary time.

But how did we do ordinary things? What did we eat? How did we travel? How did we get our news? What did we do for fun? Where did we live? How did we actively support the war effort? How did we keep in touch, and support each other?

There were restrictions. First, there was rationing of sugar, butter, coffee and meat. Sharp in my memory is the white margarine that looked like lard, sold with its little packet of food coloring to be added, and adding the color did make the butter substitute more acceptable. In general, I do not remember ever being hungry. In hindsight, we managed well and did not feel deprived. Some would say we didn't miss a thing. In fact, the thing to do was to have a victory garden in the backyard and can and freeze the produce, which my mother did.

Second, there were travel restrictions. Gasoline was rationed for essential and non-essential uses. Our cars carried a sticker with either an "A," or a "B," or a "T." Local buses had only recently replaced trolley cars. To go to the Country Club for an afternoon of swimming and tennis, we took buses from the other end of town and walked the final two miles up hill, repeating the pattern for the return trip. I went back and forth to Middlebury College in Vermont on crowded trains, often sitting on my suitcase in the aisle. Also, when I went to Middlebury in September, I did not come home again until Christmas. Public transportation was alive and well, with buses for local destinations, trains for long-distance trips.

How did we actively support the war effort? I felt encouraged to stay in college to complete the four-year liberal-arts program I was enrolled in. Middlebury College is and was a coed college, but by the end of my sophomore year, most of the male students had left and a Navy V-12 unit had arrived. Essentially the coed college became a women's college. All the leadership roles were filled by women. The college calendar shifted to year-round programs, and a Red Cross home- nursing course was required. That is where I first learned to give and receive glorious backrubs. Truckloads of college students became the labor force for getting local Vermont apples to market. My class of 1945 graduated three different times, in October '44, February '45 and June '45.

Civilians were enlisted as plane spotters. When in York, on Saturday mornings from 6-10 a.m., my mother, sister, another friend, and I would go downtown to a control center (an upstairs room in the Knights of Columbus building) to play bridge, eat candy, smoke cigarettes, and otherwise be on call should a plane be spotted from Pleasureville Hill on the outskirts of town.

In the neighborhood I remember the blackout curtains, air raid drills and the block patrol—a neighbor walking the beat to check for any light showing through anyone's windows. I volunteered at the Red Cross, rolling bandages and contacting the families of released prisoners. We entertained servicemen at USO (United Services Organization) parties, dancing to records in the York County Academy gymnasium. Picture all of us jitterbugging to the "Boogie Woogie Bugle Boy of Company B."

Housing was tight. My sister married in 1943, and they lived with my parents until the end of the war. We got our news from the radio and newspapers and from the newsreels at the movies. And we wrote daily letters to friends and sweethearts away from home.

We all remember where we were on special days in our national life. On Pearl Harbor Day, Bruce, my future husband, phoned me at Middlebury from Williams College. We were both freshmen. The day President Roosevelt died in April 1945 I burst into tears when I came upon my little sister, then 12 years old. She had been born in 1932 and had known no other President in her lifetime. On V-J Day there were spontaneous parades. People just took their cars and got into the parade!

Bruce phoned me from Tucson Ariz., on D-Day, June 6, 1944. A long-distance call in those days was a big deal. Calls were routed through regional operators across the country. He told me that he and his crew would soon be picking up a new four-engine plane to fly into combat. He would not know until opening the sealed orders in flight whether he was being sent to the Pacific or to Europe. If he was being sent to Europe, he told me that in a few days he would fly over my family's house.

Sure enough, a few days later a shiny new Liberator bomber, a B-24, did fly over my house. My brother-in-law and I grabbed a big white sheet and rushed out into the yard, hoping for another pass. It came! We flapped and flapped our big white sheet and waved joyously, absolutely thrilled with our sendoff.

In ensuing correspondence I kept asking Bruce how it was for him. He avoided, ignored and otherwise refused to answer my questions. Not until he returned to the States in June 1945 did he ever tell me that it was not he who flew over my house that day. So who knows who got such a glorious sendoff? Someone did.

In the end, what we did for one, we did for all. We were all in it together.

A native of York, Pa., Mary Elizabeth, a graduate of Middlebury College, published author and prize-winning knitter, served as Head Master's Wife at The Lawrenceville School for 27 years, volunteering on the boards of several community service organizations in New Jersey and New Hampshire. She and her husband Bruce are the parents of three children.

The Lighting Designer

Robert W. McKinley

When the war began, I was living in New Jersey and working for Westinghouse Electric as a lighting engineer. Although I had applied for a commission in the Navy, it had not yet been granted when, in May 1942, I was sent as a civilian by Westinghouse to work on a project for Captain Hyman Rickover at the Bureau of Ships. Along with another Westinghouse engineer and two from General Electric, our task was to develop a very secret method of interior lighting which would not reveal a ship's location at night.

After developing this lighting method, we engineers had to go out on Navy ships to make sure that the installations were correct and worked properly. From my wife Brownie's point-of-view, I would "disappear" for three or four days on this kind of assignment. This continued until March 1944, when I "disappeared" for three months. Brownie received a package containing my civilian clothes but no indication of where I was. (The Navy provided me with a uniform so that I would not be considered a spy in case of capture.) I was in the Pacific working on another project with Admiral Rickover, but that did not become known until later.

In 1945, after the atom bomb was used, I decided to resign and returned to New York where I edited the first edition of a handbook for the Illuminating Engineering Society. I managed to do this only because there was not yet a policy in place regarding assigned civilians. Some of my fellow engineers who delayed resigning were eventually subject to military policy and had to wait to return to civilian life.

Even though the war was over, the Navy kept insisting that the lighting project was still secret until Life magazine published an article about it.

—Contributed by Brownie McKinley

A native of Lowell, Mass., Bob attended Lowell High School, Mount Hermon School and the Massachusetts Institute of Technology. An expert on lighting and glass, Bob began his career working at Sylvania, Westinghouse and IES and eventually became director of technical services for PPG Industries in Pittsburgh. He served as an elder in his church and on the boards of many technical organizations. He and his wife Brownie have three daughters.

Meeting That Special One

Irene Peacock Moore

On December 7, 1941, I was sixteen years old and living in Garden City, Long Island, N.Y. I remember so clearly being together with my whole family, which was always a must on a Sunday. I believe we had finished Sunday dinner and were all sitting around listening to the big wooden radio with its big tuning knobs. The program was interrupted with the news that Pearl Harbor's army and naval bases had been attacked by Japanese planes. Our President, Franklin Roosevelt, came on to verify the news and we declared war on Japan.

My brother became a pilot of a B-17 bomber named "The Magnificent Obsession." He flew across the Atlantic with his crew of nine who became like brothers. They were based on the east coast of England and flew 35 missions over Germany, bombing factories and bases at first. Then they were ordered to bomb cities and he felt so guilty to think he was undoubtedly killing innocent people.

For the next three years I knitted socks and mittens for the Red Cross. I also was an Airplane Spotter in a tower near the Army Air Force base at Mitchell Field, but I never did see any enemy planes. When I was 18 my two older sisters and I went to USO dances to entertain the boys.

In June of 1943 I graduated from the Cathedral School of Saint Mary, an Episcopal girls' school. We of course had a prom which made it necessary to have a date. I invited an older brother of one of my best friends. He consented, and while dancing he said, "We're going to a party after this." I hesitated, not knowing the hostess well. We had to walk in the dark, as car headlights were dimmed by painting the top of the headlights black. We entered the kitchen where most of the guests had gathered. There were eight midshipmen from Columbia University, called 90-day wonders, having just graduated from college and signed up to enter the Navy.

There, leaning on the table was a very happy, smiling boy. He had just graduated from Williams College, class of 1943, as had my prom partner. The boy's name was Harold C. Moore, Jr., known by all as Chub. We chatted and laughed and of course I flirted. He later became my husband. When it was time to leave some of his buddies were sleeping on the floor in the living room. They had all missed the last Long Island Railroad train back to New York. So I invited Chub and two of his friends to come home with me. They accepted, so off we went. When we got to the main avenue I saw a dimly lit car in the distance. I told the boys to hide behind the trees and as the car approached I stood out and put my thumb out. The gentleman stopped and I called the boys from behind the trees and we all hopped in his car. It was a short ride, we thanked him profusely, and we arrived home safely. Two of my sisters who had also been at the party had come home with another two midshipmen. We had three empty bedrooms on the third floor. My mother said, "If you make the beds, they may stay."

That night Chub invited me to go to the "Prairie State" Graduation Ball with him. Of course no 18-year old would say "No." My mother said I could go and arrangements were made for me to stay with my aunt in New York. It was a wonderful evening and Chub was a marvelous dancer. I certainly was becoming very interested in him. For the next several weeks, we dated in town, doing Greenwich Village and the uptown nightclubs, going to the beach.

The middle of July came and we parted. Chub went to Evansville, Indiana to board his ship, the *LST 246*, as a gunnery officer. The ship would be his home for ... no one knew how long. The ship was involved in the Marshall Islands invasions, and a description of these events, as told by Bill Askin, the Captain's Talker on the bridge, can be found on Page 139.

Following the war, *LST 246* performed occupation duty in the Far East until early February 1946 when she returned to the United States and was decommissioned on 14 February 1946. On 26 June 1947 she was transferred to the United States Army and struck from the Navy list on 12 March 1948. *LST 246* earned six battle stars for World War II service.

In the meantime, I wanted to go to art school in New York, but mother put her foot down and said, "No daughter of mine is going to art school and end up as a Bohemian in Greenwich Village, and that 's that!" So, I went to Mrs. Skinner's Secretarial School in Garden City. I accelerated and finished in one year (1944).

I got a job at Conde Nast Publishers. They published House & Garden, Glamour, Vogue and Vogue Pattern Books. I worked for the Art Director Editor, Caroline Bedard, of Vogue Pattern Books. I loved choosing fabrics to go with different patterns, and seeing the making of the clothes for fashion shows in all the better department stores across the United States. We had representatives that put on the shows. I worked there until March 1946 when I left to be married.

Chub arrived in San Francisco on July 30, 1945, for a 30-day leave. His orders were to return to his ship after it was refitted for the invasion of Tokyo. My family moved to Brooklyn Heights, N.Y., on July 25th. I was beside myself with fear Chub would not be able to find me because we had not been able to correspond for about four weeks. On August 1st I received a telegram from him at my office. "Meet me under clock at Biltmore 5 p.m. Aug. 3." Of course I was excited and of course I was there! We had a good cheer toast, dinner, and visited the old haunts. When we decided to go home to Brooklyn at 2 a.m. it was almost impossible to get a taxi because the taxi driver would find it difficult to pick up a passenger on the way back to Manhattan. One very nice man saw Chub in his Navy uniform, took pity on us and drove us back to Brooklyn.

Chub spent two nights and then went home to West Newton, Mass., to find his father recuperating from a heart attack. They hadn't told Chub as they didn't want him to worry. I was about to start a two- week vacation when I was invited to visit his home to meet his family.

On the 6th of August 1945, the United States dropped the atomic bomb on Tokyo. Nobody had ever heard of the A-bomb and because of the tremendous destruction and loss of life, the Japanese surrendered at once.

Chub came back to spend a week with me before he returned to his ship on at the end of August. On the 2nd of September 1945 the war was officially over when the Americans and Japanese met on the U.S.S. *Missouri* in Tokyo Harbor and signed the surrender documents. Chub called me that night and asked, "Will you marry me?"

and I immediately said, "Yes!"

Chub finally came home for good the 1st of April, 1946. After much planning we were married at St. Bartholomew's Episcopal Church on April 27, 1946. We of course hired limousines to take the wedding party to the reception at The Cosmopolitan Club. The red light turned green, we pulled out, and suddenly we were hit broadside by a beer truck! We came to a very abrupt stop! The car was smoking and the driver couldn't open his door. Someone got us out.

After the reception — dancing to Lester Lanin we said farewell to our families and guests. Chub's father handed him the keys to a new, just-off-the-assembly-line Plymouth sedan, which was to be Chub's business car. We drove to the Plaza to spend a week before driving South. We had only had champagne, a few goodies and a piece of wedding cake at the reception, so we ordered ham and cheese sandwiches and champagne on ice to be sent up to the room.

The next morning I woke up to the loudest noise in the bathroom. I thought something had gotten loose from the Central Park Zoo! But no, it was Chub being deathly ill. He came out looking the color green and plopped onto the bed. Twenty minutes later I made hasty tracks to the john and I was deathly sick also.

At 9:30 I called my mother to ask her if anybody had called to say they were ill. She was horrified but later reported back that nobody else was ill. We later learned that "Hildegard," the well-known entertainer who played the piano wearing white gloves, was sick and had to cancel her programs. Well, we had to cancel our plans as well. The ham in the sandwiches had given us food poisoning.

After three days we requested more toilet paper. When the chambermaid came in with a stack of six packages she looked around at confetti and rice all over the floor. As she left we heard her say to her partner, "Honeymoon couple are still in bed after three days." At least we didn't spend much money on meals ... just one dinner and tea and toast.

We drove south and, having not completely recovered, we were forced to stop about every 50 miles to use the facilities at run-down, unkempt, antique, dirty gas stations. There were no modern highways yet; we passed many shabby houses.

When we finally got to Savannah, Ga., Chub changed into

his Navy uniform ... now a full lieutenant ... and entered the Cloisters at Sea Island. We had a fabulous honeymoon. After almost two weeks Chub went to pay the bill with his "Terminal Leave" check for $320. The clerk gave him one nickel back in change ... and the honeymoon was over.

A native of Garden City, N.Y., on Long Island, Irene attended the Catholic School of St. Mary and Mrs. Skinners Secretarial School and worked as a professional embroiderer, teacher, interior designer and restorer. She and her husband, the late Harold C. Moore, Jr., had four children.

SHELTERED FROM THE STORM

EDITH V. PARKER

After the attack on Pearl Harbor, I experienced the war as a teen-aged girl. A relative was called up to serve with his National Guard unit in North Africa.

Our town organized a "Victory Corps" through the school district and we held student rallies. We were all fingerprinted—we assumed for expedited identification of casualties in the event of massive bombing. We used to find various pieces of flotsam and jetsam on the beaches of our vacation home, which we imagined indicated submarine warfare just offshore. And, of course, there was the rationing to civilians of items in short supply or high demand, due to the priority for military use.

I grew up in suburbia, sheltered and protected. My family consisted of my widowed mother and a sister seven years older. We weathered the Depression thanks to my father's foresight.

Born in Toledo, Ohio, Edith was raised in South Orange, N.J. She earned her bachelor's and Master's degrees at Syracuse University and worked in social work during her career. She volunteered for a number of civic organizations, including the Girl Scouts, League of Women Voters, the American Association of University Women and the Woman's Society of the United Church of Christ (Congregational). She and her late husband Harold had two children.

Uranium and Spies

Margo Potter

In June 1942 I graduated from St. Lawrence University in upstate New York. My future husband, James A. (Jack) Potter was taking summer courses, hoping to enter medical school at the University of Rochester School of Medicine. However, his draft board could not fill its quota and Jack was drafted. The Medical School dean interceded and Jack entered the first class to finish in three years instead of four. A couple of months later the medical schools were taken over by the Army and Navy, and required every qualified student to be drafted. In June 1944 students were allowed to be married, and on June 21, 1944 we took our vows, as did many of the students.

Behind the hospital the government built a secret experimental laboratory to learn about uranium: how much radioactivity was absorbed under working conditions and where it settled in the body. I was hired to work in this facility. When I was finally cleared by security I was told in secret the name of the substance I had previously known only as "T." We found an accurate way to test uranium. We then exposed mice to known amounts to learn where it was settling in the body.

When Jack received his medical degree he had to stay in the Navy two more years. He was ordered to the Jacksonville, Fla., Naval Air Base. He worked in the hospital there for 16 months, and then was sent to San Diego, Calif., as medical director for three destroyer escorts. He was able to live at home, off base.

When the war ended, he was just marking time before beginning his specialty studies in surgery in San Francisco. He was called back during the Korean Conflict, but stayed in San Francisco and could live at home.

After I graduated from college I took a course in typing and office machines. I then went to Rochester and worked for Dunn and Bradstreet on a security project involving reports on the employees of government war projects. There were two gentlemen who were working with me and gathering the information that I was to write up in a report to the Dunn and Bradstreet clients. These men were elderly in appearance and not highly motivated.

They certainly couldn't and didn't uncover any spies or foreign agents who wished to be hidden. I was left with using my imagination in making my reports individual. In looking back, I feel this was a useless project and waste of money. It could have been exciting.

Margo was born in Cortland, N.Y. She attended the Northfield Seminary, and St. Lawrence University. She and her husband, Dr. James A. Potter, raised three children.

Boot Camp in the Bronx

Hazel S. Quick

On July 2, 1944, I was on a bus traveling from Colusa, Calif., to Sacramento in order to enlist in a U.S. Naval Reserve branch for women known as WAVES (Women Accepted for Volunteer Emergency Service). Women over 18 but not yet 21 years old needed parental consent. A Naval recruiter in San Jose had given me information about this branch. School was out for the summer at San Jose State College where I had just finished my junior year. The battles of World War II were raging fiercely. My patriotism was aroused. I decided to enlist. My parents gave their consent.

Having accomplished my mission, I returned home to Colusa to await further instructions for my departure to boot camp at Hunter College in the Bronx, N.Y. Late in July my father drove me to Davis and I boarded a troop train especially for WAVES and began a new adventure.

After leaving Davis we were soon out of the Valley, up and over the Sierra Nevada Mountains and through the snow sheds that protected the railroad tracks from the twelve-foot winter snowfall. We continued through Nevada and Utah, over the Rockies to the prairies, the Great Plains and into the Midwest. We were headed for Chicago, that wonderful city on Lake Michigan where we would change trains and continue on to New York.

When we reached Chicago there was a long delay as we waited for the other train to form a new group of cars for our troop train. Some of us rushed to the Marshall Fields department store to shop and others chose to enjoy that marvelous park by Lake Michigan. What an oasis that is in the midst of a huge city! Finally all was arranged and the taxis collected all of us and sped across the cobblestoned streets to the other train.

We had left California at the height of its brown summer season, but now the world turned into a gorgeous Kelly green. The sights were wonderful. By the time we came to the Mohawk River I decided New York State was the most beautiful. We turned south and roared on down along the Hudson River and suddenly there it was, New York, the city that was home to seven million people.

We had arrived and been given the gift of seeing our country from sea to shining sea! We arrived at Grand Central Station. Everyone rushed off the train and "marched," if you can call it that, to the subway that would take us non-stop to the Bronx. At the end of a fast ride we found a beautiful uncluttered campus with stately stone buildings. Here was the elegant Hunter College, our boot camp!

Boot camp accommodations for new recruits were in the six-story apartment buildings surrounding the campus. The apartments in the house I was assigned to consisted of two rooms and one bath, each unit housing 10 women. Six of us were in the largest room with three double bunks, and in the smallest room were four with two double bunks. I can't remember where we put our clothes. The place was packed. We quickly learned to gracefully share our space and not to linger in the bath.

Immediately we were sent through a series of physical and mental tests to confirm that we were of suitable size and weight and had enough physical and mental stamina to perform our duties for the US Navy. We were given shots for everything possible. We were still dressed in our civilian clothes except we wore sensible shoes, long, hot, cotton hose and snap-brimmed hats. Uniform fitting would come later, after we had been considered adequate. We were a motley crew.

We exercised, learned to march and immediately obey commands, give a snappy salute to our superiors, use Navy lingo for certain things, and always when we marched, keep the same cadence as all the others in the platoon. To do all these things while marching we sang to the top of our lungs and finally marched in the Saturday Regimental Reviews.

In our classrooms we studied U.S. Naval history, math, and were constantly tested to be sure we learned it all, including the chain of command, the duties of various officers, etc., and all things about the Navy. The college buildings were connected by underground passages wide enough to march 12 abreast. We were up with the birds and kept very busy. We never walked alone. We marched in all types of weather, back and forth from the campus to the apartments, to meals, to church, and even to the subway. There was no fooling around.

It was a hot summer and along came a hurricane that turned trees upside down and rain poured in through the skylight on the sixth floor. Our room was on the fifth floor. During the storm we kept marching: to class, to meals, and back again. Our raincoats survived nicely, but our shoes were never the same again. We now had new uniforms for winter and summer. We were issued two of all clothing items except only one raincoat that had a nice warm lining good enough for any weather.

It seemed like a constant whirr as new and interesting events occurred. The drinking water made me ill, and some of my fellow recruits reacted to the shots that were given and fainted while marching. Some were sent home and the rest of us were destined for more training elsewhere. Those who already had skills that the Navy could use were sent directly to their new duties. None of us were given foreign assignments beyond the 48 states. After six weeks, boot camp was finally over. My sister Audrey, who was a WAC, came to view our final Regimental Review. I had one day off. She was the snappiest looking soldier and I was proud to be seen with her in New York City.

My destination was the Georgia State College for Women in the town of Milledgeville, where training for store keepers would take place. Milledgeville is in the heart of Georgia. During the 1860s it had briefly been the state Capital when Georgia seceded from the Union. Every Saturday we marched at the Military Academy Campus parade grounds which are on the very grounds of the old Capital. The main building has been restored to its original condition. Sherman did not burn this town on his way to the sea. The cemeteries were full of Confederate flags. Georgia had suffered mightily.

I was from the Far West and this was all very new to me. The town was segregated even for those walking on the sidewalks. The red clay soil of Georgia clung to my black shoes when it rained but I learned how to get a new shine on them in spite of the red mud. I also discovered how delicious the pecans of Georgia were that fell from the huge pecan trees on the campus.

We were up at 5:30 in the morning, in bed at 9:30 at night and spent our days in classes. The program lasted from early September until late December and the heat of fall turned into the cold of winter. Finally we finished our training and were designated Store Keepers Third Class. Now it was time to be sent to take care of supplies or disbursements at our new destinations.

We were given choices of bases that needed personnel and I chose San Francisco. This time I was on a troop train with just six WAVES going back to California. The rest were sailors on their way to duty in the Pacific. The troop trains took their time crossing the country. We sat on the sidings a lot letting faster trains steam ahead. On my trip down to Georgia I had not carefully packed my suitcase, and one of the sleeves on my nightgown had arrived blackened from the soot from the trains. This time I made sure nothing was fluttering in the breeze outside of my suitcase.

Passing through Kentucky and Tennessee in the night caused me not to see the land. I can say I have been there but my eyes have not seen these two states. The winter scenes of red barns, white snow and small towns are still vivid in my mind. Again I marveled at the sights of winter as we traveled west. Finally, just before Christmas 1944, we arrived back in California.

My destination in San Francisco was the Bureau of Yards and Docks that had offices on Market and 3rd Streets. We handled the manifests for the shipments to the Pacific of materials needed by the Construction Battalions in order to build new bases. These sailors were known as "CBs." We also sent supplies for the ships fighting the war at sea. Every destination had a secret code name. The harbor was full of ships. We worked 8 a.m. to 5 p.m.

My hometown of Colusa was just 110 miles away but I wasn't allowed to travel more than 50 miles from the base. I could not go home for Christmas. There was a war going on! A friend of mine from San Jose invited me to stay at her house the night before Christmas. Her family had also taken in another sailor. We were treated to a Swedish Christmas.

The mother of my friend was a singer. She had prepared a Christmas Eve supper but before the supper we all went to church and she sang the beautiful Santa Lucia song in Swedish as she walked the length of the church with lit candles in her long, fair hair. After the service we had a huge feast in the middle of the night. The kindness of that family has stayed with me all these years. People were very generous to those in the service.

My favorite places in San Francisco were the Golden Gate Park and the docks where I had a close up view of all the ships coming and going. The aircraft carrier U.S.S. Boxer made it into port in spite of a huge hole under the front of the flight deck.

Since there were no barracks for women in San Francisco at that time the Navy took over the Western Women's Club, a ten-story building below Nob Hill located at the corner of Sutter and Mason. There were more than 600 of us there. A single room with a bath became room for four. Even the ballroom was filled with double bunks. There were four of us in one room on the ninth floor with two double bunks, one dresser and a closet. I can't remember if there was a chair since I didn't have time to sit in it. Every evening I could look out at the top of Nob Hill and hear the chimes of the Grace Cathedral ring. I'd sit on my knees by the window listening to the beautiful music and feel grateful for such luxury. There was even a swimming pool in the basement.

As soon as the war ended in August 1945 the Bureau of Yards and Docks shut up like a clam. The battleship U.S.S. Alabama came back into port in good shape after nine successful battles. The lights came on again after many years of blackout and "The City," as northern Californians called San Francisco, celebrated. I was transferred to the Federal Building where we kept records of the ships present in the harbor. I walked everywhere day or night. The street cars and cable cars were happily clanging away. The United Nations were meeting and there were people from all over the world on the street. We all were allowed to witness the signing of the UN Charter at an appointed time.

Finally I had enough points to get discharged. They asked me to sign up again but I said, "No, thank you," and sent my transcript to the University of California in Berkeley. Early in May 1946 I received an honorable discharge. With my clothing allowance of $200 I bought a coat and four dresses. I had two pairs of shoes. My mother made a white blouse for me and I changed the buttons on my uniform jacket and altered the lapels, removed the insignia, kept the two uniform skirts, bought a sweater and socks and enrolled in the University of California, Berkeley.

There was lodging available at the International House where I lived for two years. Its motto was "That Brotherhood May Prevail," and there were people from 56 nations living there. After those long years of war, I appreciated all those newfound friends, both international and from across the country that I made.

I am grateful to my country for the wonderful kindness of the GI Bill for veterans of a terrible war, and for allowing me to serve.

A native of Seattle, Wash., Hazel graduated from the University of California at Berkeley and was a school teacher early in her career. After raising three children with her husband Elwyn B. Quick, she worked as vice president for the Publishers Storage and Shipping Corp.

HELPING WITH THE JANGOS

EVELYN SCHMITT

During the war in my hometown of Washington, D.C., I became a JANGO (Junior Army-Navy Guild Organization). JANGOs were teenagers (14-18 years old) who helped out in war work.

The most popular activity was the junior nurses' aide at Doctor's Hospital. Other projects included rolling bandages at Walter Reed Hospital, helping at the Red Cross Day Nursery in Constitution Hall, serving as "canteen' girls" at the Soliders, Sailors and Marines Club, plus groups that went to Walter Reed's Convalescent Hospital at Forest Glen to take part in square dancing events.

Until I went off to college, I participated on a regular basis in the nurses' aide project and the Soldiers, Sailors and Marines Club Canteen. At the hospital, we had minor duties like bed pans and water and tray service. Training was provided for more advanced chores. These activities made me feel I was helping the war effort in some way. JANGOs received quite a bit of recognition, even a cover story in Life Magazine.

Later, as a college student at the College of William and Mary in Virginia, I expressed my thoughts and feelings on V-E Day, in this essay:

> Of the many special occasions and gala events that I will always remember of my college days, there is one simple ceremony that I shall never forget. It was a little before noon on May 7, 1945. Students gathered on the west side of the Wren building for the outside convocation. Some found spots to relax on the green lawn; others stood against the ivy-clad walls and picket fences.
>
> Forming a wall to the west, in which direction lies Ja-

pan, were the naval chaplains, who stood at attention. On all this, the sun beamed gloriously.

This was the setting for which I experienced the first victory I have ever known. Although it was only a partial victory, all at once and only for a moment, peace seemed to reign again.

A native of Washington, D.C., Evelyn attended the College of William & Mary, George Washington University and Gwynedd Mercy College. She worked in human resource management for UNISYS throughout her career, retiring in 1984. She has four children.

BUMPED

NAN SHOLL

The DC-3 labored to cross the Sierras on the first leg of its flight from Seattle to Newark, N. J., early in April of 1945. My enjoyment of the beauty of the landscape below was clouded by thoughts of what I was leaving and of what lay ahead.

Cal and I had been married just a few weeks earlier and spent our honeymoon aboard a train traveling from New York to Seattle. A newly commissioned ensign, Cal had been assigned to a ship being built in Tacoma, Wash. Housing was difficult to find but we had finally located a room rental in the home of a delightful elderly lady looking for companionship after her own family had been called into service. We looked forward to at least two months of "marital bliss" before his ship was launched and destined to sail for the South Pacific. But I received a call that my mother was gravely ill and I was needed at home.

As the plane made its bumpy way aloft, I could not help but think of the events leading up to our marriage. There was December 7th, the exodus of men from Bucknell, Cal's enlistment in the Navy's V-12 program, a campus converted to training enlisted Navy recruits, food and gas rationing, blackouts, air raid drills, first aid training, our engagement and my graduation, which I skipped so that I could plan a wedding before Cal was sent overseas. Whatever hardships or inconveniences we experienced then were nothing compared to the sacrifices being made by service personnel in the battles of Europe and the Pacific.

My thoughts were interrupted as we jolted to a landing in Billings, Mont., the first leg of the trip east. Expecting a short layover, I was distraught to learn that I was being "bumped" because of the wartime policy: service personnel had priority over civilians. I had to spend the night in Billings and the following morning ventured outside the hotel where I was greeted by every "cowboy" that passed with a warm "good morning ma'am" and a tip of a hat. The attention made me uncomfortable and with my Eastern mentality, I wondered if looked "fast" or somehow inappropriate. Only later did I realize that I was the recipient of the famous warmth and friendliness of the "blue sky" country.

I was able to get on a plane from Billings to Fargo, N. Dak.. But here again I was bumped to make room for service personnel, a policy with which I was in full agreement. After the next leg to Minneapolis, I was again bumped and concluded the train to Newark was my only option.

I found my mother failing rapidly. After spending a lot of precious time with her, she insisted that I go back to the West Coast to see Cal before he left for the South Pacific. This time I opted to travel by train to San Diego on the Atchison, Topeka and Santa Fe. The trip was arduous but the objective discounted any miseries of travel. Cal and I had a happy reunion but on the day of my arrival I received word that my mother had died. Shortly thereafter Cal started his voyage to the Philippine Islands where his ship would supply advanced bases and participate in the upcoming invasion of Japan.

I returned to my home in New Jersey, a job on the Lower East Side of New York as a YWCA International Center Youth Director and an anxious wait for the end of the war. My responsibilities at the Center were to organize and direct activities for young people in that "tough" neighborhood.

Whatever the social or ethical ramifications at that time of dropping the bomb that ended the war, I was among those overjoyed to see the war come to an end. Cal was among the fortunate ones to return unscathed and we went back to Bucknell, where he had one semester to complete before graduating.

Participating in the transformation of the campus back from a "military" establishment was delightful. Living on the hill overlooking the Susquehanna River and the mountains beyond certainly beat the view of Third Avenue in New York City. Life was good and we had so much for which to be thankful.

Born and raised in Chatham, N.J., Nan graduated from Bucknell University. After graduation and marriage to Cal she was preoccupied with raising her four children and serving on her town's planning and conservation boards, working with the Girl Scouts and volunteering at her local hospital.

Actors on the Deck

Sidney A. Walker

I enlisted in the Navy in December 1942 and took officer's training at Smith College. I was then sent to Washington to serve in the convoy and routing section.

This was an ideal post for keeping an eye on the destroyer on which Winthrop Walker, my future husband, was serving as it convoyed tankers to and from the Gulf.

I got permission from Admiral King to wear a wedding dress on September 17, 1943. Five months later, I received a medical discharge with a large safety pin in the waistline of my uniform.

When I joined the Navy, I took over for the many men who were sent to active duty. I was on duty one evening when Douglas Fairbanks Jr. and James Cagney strolled in to say hello to their former commander. I wondered which one I had replaced. I called everyone to attention and saluted them as they came in.

After growing up in Monclair, N.J., Sidney attended Milton Academy and Smith College. She married Winthrop Walker and after the war they lived in Cape Elizabeth, Maine. She volunteered for Family Services and the Portland Art Museum.

Defending Fishers Island

Alan Wilder

On a Sunday afternoon in December 1941 I heard about the Japanese attack on Pearl Harbor. I sat in front of the radio with my three sisters and our parents. My dad, Burl Wilder, was 41, with four children and my mother, Ernestine. He never served. He continued to work for Savin Construction Co. in Hartford, Conn., as a superintendent and ultimately retired 35 years later, at age 76, as chief engineer.

On Christmas day 1941, I was as excited as any young boy could be. I was so excited that I was riveted on the scene of the Christmas tree and all the presents. I noticed some glances between family members, but didn't understand. Finally, after all the presents were opened, I finally looked around and saw it! Leaning on the far wall in the living room was a new Elgin two-wheel bike, with the smaller diameter high-pressure tires. I had learned to ride that previous summer on my oldest sister's bike. But it was pretty creaky, and my shrewd parents, realizing that a war meant there would be fewer items like bikes available, had decided to buy me this new one.

It was a very warm Christmas that year, no snowfall yet, so I rode that bike all over town, visiting all my friends, I suspect bragging more than a little. I rode it for years, well after the war was over, until I ultimately at age 17 inherited the family car from the war years, a 1938 Chrysler Royale. I even drove that car to college.

During that first war winter the government shrewdly announced on a Sunday morning that rubber rationing would start on Monday, because nearly all stores were closed Sunday. But they neglected to consider that in some places, and Hartford was one, Jewish- owned stores typically closed on Saturday, and were open Sunday. The entire family went down to Berman's Department Store, a small store in the south end of Hartford where we did business before the war and long after. I seriously doubt if that store had ever had as good a day as that. They ran out of rubber in all sizes and shapes, galoshes, boots, raincoats and even rubber gloves.

I read a lot. We got the Hartford *Times*, an afternoon paper no longer in existence. I read about the tragedy in the Pacific in particular, through that first war winter and into spring. Then one day there was a headline I will never forget: FOUR JAP CARRIERS SUNK AT MIDWAY. We knew nothing about the meaning of this, but it was the first thing we had seen that was a positive note on the war. It was of course the turning point in the Pacific, and after that point we dominated the Pacific war, in most situations.

I was a Cub Scout and ultimately a Boy Scout, in Troop 106 in our town. We had paper and metal drives a number of times during the war. I once went to a home near us and the woman gave us about 100 pounds of National Geographic magazines. We got good money for scrap paper, and I was ready to turn the magazines in to our troop, but my Mother intervened. She figured the weight, the value, and gave me the money to turn in. We read those magazines for years and years after that. So much for the war effort!

Our Chrysler got about 18 miles per gallon, and with an A card, which we had firmly attached to the windshield corner, our weekly ration was just three gallons at the lowest point of the war. This was enough for about 50 miles, so trips anywhere were carefully scheduled. I recall few times it was a bother, but I know the family was pretty careful with traveling. The speed limits were a maximum of 45 miles per hour, everywhere, to save gas. Tires were also in short supply, and recapping originated at that time. The top half of the headlights were painted black, to minimize light at night which could be seen as a glow a long way off, such as in a submarine or bomber.

One trip we took in that car was to New London, and then we took the ferry over to Fishers Island, about seven miles off the coast. Starting late in 1942 or early 1943, Savin won a contract to build the government's gun emplacements on the island. The island had an existing fort, H.G. Wright, which had been a coastal defense fort for many years, with disappearing guns of 6-, 10- and 12-inch caliber, considered by most to be obsolete by the late 30's. Early in the war it was decided we needed to beef up the defenses along Long Island Sound. In 1943 two emplacements were built on Fisher Island, a pair for 16-inch guns and a pair of 6-inch guns. Dad was the superintendent on this job.

The emplacement for the 16-inch guns was roughly 1000 feet long, and consisted of 14-foot thick concrete covered with a thick layer of dirt. We lived on the island that summer and fall, leaving finally about Thanksgiving.

When the contract was nearly done the company was awarded an Army-Navy "E" award, for "excellence," and a ceremony was held, with speeches and all. The contract cost I believe was about $3 million. The guns were never installed.

The island was composed of a village of several hundred people near the fort, and the balance of the island, 90% or more, was owned by a small number of very wealthy families. Most of the villagers normally worked for these families as housekeepers, maids, yardmen or caretakers. But in 1943 the Navy effectively took over the island, and unless you lived there permanently you could not go "on island" at all. So Savin rented a large house "up island" for us, and the Navy gave us each a permit to go out. That way Dad was able to put in longer work weeks, and make better progress on the project.

The work force was a bit unusual also, since so many able-bodied men were not available. My uncle and cousin came from Cleveland to work that summer, and stayed in the house with us. It was no problem, since the house had a lot of bedrooms, but cooking was endless for my mother. Savin had also rented a large barn on the island and equipped it for their employees with beds and a kitchen. Except for weekends, this is where most of the help stayed and ate.

There was a small grocery store on the island, where almost everyone shopped. There were price controls in effect, so nobody would overly profit from the war economy. Prices had been frozen at the level they had been just before the war, with a few exemptions. That was fine with the grocery store owner on the island: he had aways upped his prices for the wealthy summer crowd. So when they froze his prices, it was at that high level year-round! He did quite nicely during the war. Meat was always a rarity due to rationing. Mom found she could stuff a beef heart and bake it, and we had that occasionally. It was rather tough, and I remember it well, and not fondly.

There was a one-armed lobsterman on the island, and we often bought lobster from him. I believe the price then was 45 cents a pound, which she always thought was five cents too much. But, we still ate a lot of lobster. Since Mother seldom knew much ahead of time how many would be there for dinner, this could pose a problem on lobster nights. But she was proficient at separating a lobster from its shell, having learned the trick from a woman who had worked in a lobster processing plant. She found a recipe that we still make, involving lobster, its juice, Ritz crackers and a little salt and pepper, and at that time not butter but margarine. It worked nicely when there were nine lobsters and eleven people. More Ritz crackers always helped!

The movie theater on the post had two showings, one early that non-military residents could go to, and a later one just for the military. So dinner was sometimes hurried, and off we went to the show. One perk we enjoyed was that we could buy one of the large Hershey bars for just 25 cents. Chocolate was very scarce, so we took advantage of this whenever we could.

The concerns about enemy submarines had lessened some by this time in the war. However, we still had specific rules about lights at night. Our shades were always drawn at dusk. One night, being a typically curious youngster, I raised and lowered the shade, all in a split second, just to see what would happen. Nothing happened, of course, and I'm not sure what I was expecting. A shelling? A torpedo shot up onto the lawn? (We were half a mile inland!) There was a scary story going around at that time, probably rumor only, that a German submarine had been sunk just off the coast, and that the debris coming to the surface included loaves of bread, three days old, made in New London.

We had the beach to explore when the weather was nice, and went there often. For entertainment at night there was only the radio and sometimes a newspaper my Father had picked up somewhere during the day, which someone had brought over on the ferry from New London. So we played a lot cards, read a lot, and my Mother played the piano.

I started sixth grade that year in the island school, which had two rooms. I was worried about that, since it was a New York system, reputedly tougher than the Connecticut schools. It was true, but when we returned to Wethersfield about Thanksgiving time I had about a two or three week jump on my classmates there, so sometimes you come out ahead.

At night in Wethersfield it was usually quiet after I went to bed. But if the window was open I could hear, a few miles away, the .50 caliber machine guns being tested at Colts. With companies like Colts Firearms, Pratt & Whitney aircraft engines and Hamilton Standard propellers in the area, we always believed we would be a prime target for German air raids. But that, of course, never happened. Early in the war we got blackout curtains, but I frankly have little recollection of them ever being used at all.

After V-E day in the spring of 1945, and the end of school that year, we went back to our summer camp in Suffield, Conn., which was on a stream, about three miles from Bradley air field. At that time it was still a military base. A captain and his wife were living at the camp in one of the cottages usually occupied by another couple, who now were somewhere else since the husband was in the service. Housing was always a problem for military couples, so even a summer cottage was useful. This captain was a flight instructor at Bradley. Again, chocolate was available on the base, but not in any civilian store. So I gave him $1.20 to buy a whole box of Hershey bars, 24 in all, and I enjoyed them slowly, over many months. I was not at all generous with them.

That summer the B-17 and B-24 bombers returned from Europe. Bradley Field was one of the first stops in the U.S. after they refueled in Gander, Newfoundland. The planes were stripped of machine guns and other unnecessary weight and in addition to the normal crew of ten men as many ground crew were loaded on as they dared.

By late morning or early afternoon these planes were coming in over our house, banking for a final approach. They were low, and I could see the markings, the bombs painted on the sides for each mission flown, and even airmen peering out the side gunners windows, and waving to us. Sometimes they were coming in just a minute apart. I can never forget that.

The Red Cross met each plane, and gave each man what he craved most: a quart of milk, something they had scarcely seen for many months.

Alan was born in Maine and grew up in Wethersfield, Conn., until leaving for college in 1950. He studied metallurgical engineering at Rensselaer Polytechnic Institute and earned his Master's degree in Industrial Administration at Union College in Schenectady, N.Y. After an early career in the nuclear industry, he owned Green Mountain Log Homes in Chester, Vt. He also held several positions in the Log Home Council of the United States, including president. He and his wife Elizabeth have three children.

The Warrior from Pan Am

John J. Young

Although I never served any time on active duty in the military during World War II, I was actively flying as a civilian for the services as a pilot for Pan American Airways, first on trans-Atlantic passenger service, followed by flights for the Navy Air Transport Command, and finally for the Army Air Corp Transport Service.

It all began in my junior year at Long Island University in Brooklyn, N.Y. I signed on to a government pilot-training program sponsored by the CAA, which was a forerunner of today's FAA. After I earned my private license, flying Piper Cubs out of Floyd Bennet Field, I enrolled in additional courses starting with flight acrobatics. At that point a decision had to be made. In order to continue in more advanced courses I would be required to drop out of my senior year at LIU. Needless to say, despite my father's being very unhappy about my decision, I continued my flight training.

I went on to get my flight instructor rating as well as my instrument flight and multi-engine rating. All this qualified me to be an airline co-pilot. Since all this was at government expense we had very little say about our future. Instead, each graduate was assigned to one of the airlines. It was my good fortune to be sent to Pan American.

I reported to work at Pan Am at LaGuardia Field in Queens, N.Y. This was fortunate since I could live with my family in Highland Park, Brooklyn, and use public transportation to commute.

I started my career with Pan Am in Ground School studying flight procedures and celestial navigation. This was followed by a 10-day stint in the hangar working with the mechanics to learn the intricacies of maintenance procedures. Then came training flights on the giant Boeing B-314 flying boats, the largest ever built for passenger service. The flight deck was 20 feet long with separate work stations for each active crew member. Because the flights could be as long as 24 hours non-stop, we had a multiple crew. In addition to the captain, there were three co-pilots, two flight engineers, two radio operators, and a single navigator whose job was not continuous. In those days there was voice communications only locally around the terminals.

Most of the communication when flying across the ocean was in Morse Code and during wartime encoded for secrecy. The B-314 was the most luxurious plane built to that time. In addition to the crew quarters where off-duty crew members could rest, there was a complete galley where restaurant-style meals could be prepared and served in the main dining salon. The seating compartments could be converted for sleeping with Pullman-style bunks. In the very rear was a private suite with its own lavatory. It earned the name of the Honeymoon Suite.

All of this was during pre-war service. Once we entered World War II all changed to a bare-bones austerity footing. The peace-time passenger capacity of 50 was increased to 74. Another unusual feature of the B-314 was a walkway in each wing where a flight engineer could crawl out into the wing to make minor repairs on any of the four engines while in flight. The walkway was also used on the surface where off-duty crew members could crawl out to counterbalance the effects of a strong crosswind. The cabin crew consisted of three stewards in peace time, reduced to two during the war. Female cabin attendants were not hired by Pan Am until 1946. Only twelve B-314 flying boats were ever built and none were in existence after 1950.

After two months of training I was finally assigned to my first overseas trip. It was a 30-day passenger flight leaving New York. The first stop was Bermuda; then on to the Azores, and finally to Lisbon, Portugal. From there we flew to Foynes, Ireland, at our port on the Shannon River. After four days while one of our engines was being repaired we flew back to Lisbon, and four days later we headed south to Monrovia, Liberia, with one stop on the way.

From there we headed across the South Atlantic to Natal, the eastern-most city in Brazil. The very next day we flew back to Liberia. After one day's rest it was back to Brazil. Three Atlantic crossings in four days. I later came to realize that this was not unusual for Pan Am.

All these crossings were made during daylight hours when it is more difficult to navigate than night flights where there are stars to enable you to establish positive positions. During the daytime we used dead reckoning with wind direction and velocity to determine an estimated position. All of this was before modern radar and tracking devices were available. We used the same method of navigation that seafarers had used for hundreds of years.

Leaving Natal, we flew to Belem, landing in the Amazon River, famous for piranhas. From Belem we proceeded north with stops at Trinidad, San Juan, and Bermuda before reaching New York, 30 days and 3,000 miles later. It was a typical trip on a slow flying boat. Each time we landed the junior pilots (3rd and 4th officers) became deck hands, responsible for picking up the mooring lines, not an easy job in rough waters.

Not widely known in those days was a division of Pan Am building airport runways for the U.S. military along routes they pioneered years before in anticipation of the war. This operation was never revealed to the public.

Back to my story: I made two more of those 30-day trips in addition to numerous one-day trips. While not on a trip we were training in preparation for future advancement. I made one trip as assistant navigator and earned my certificate in ocean navigation. So ended my first year with Pan Am.

Early in 1943 Pan Am was awarded a Navy contract to fly consolidated PB2Y3 flying boats for the transport command. All flight crew members were required to join the Naval Reserves. My three years of college credits earned me a commission as an ensign.

With a new plane, we all had to go through another training session during which time I received my first promotion to First Officer and Second in Command. Our flights started shortly thereafter. We used some of the same routes as the commercial operation but with different overseas terminals. Instead of Ireland and Portugal, both neutral countries, we landed in Northern Ireland and at a seaport near Casablanca in Morocco. We carried priority cargo and military passengers to and from the front lines in planes that had bare interiors with no insulation. This made them much noisier, particularly when these seaplanes made water landings. It was so bad sometimes that first time passengers thought that we had crash landed. It was quite different from the relatively quiet B-314.

The Navy operation continued for about 15 months. The majority of our flights were for about 16 days, with a smaller crew. The faster planes made for shorter flights.

In early 1944 as the war progressed in the European Theater, naval activity in the Atlantic declined. The Navy decided to end our program and move their planes to the Pacific area where there still was much naval activity. That action left our crews with a period of inactivity.

The lull turned out to be very short. As the Navy program ended, the company replaced it with a contract with the Army Air Corp to fly for their transport service. We would be flying Douglas C-54s, the military version of the airline DC-4s. These missions were similar to those of our Navy flights.

In preparation for the change to land planes from seaplanes, a group of pilots, including me, were sent to Miami, Fla., for flight training on the new aircraft. It was a nice change of scenery which lasted for about three weeks.

Back in New York, we began ferrying Army personnel across the ocean. We did make more trips across the North Atlantic than we had previously. Our east-bound trips were similar to those of the Navy. Return trips were quite different however. The planes were converted to use as ambulance planes for wounded servicemen being returned to the States. These were particularly special flights for us, creating a feeling of extra satisfaction with empathy for our passengers and appreciation of their sacrifices.

It was 1945. As spring turned into summer Louise and I married and were living in New York as I continued flying for the Army Transport Service. The war in Europe came to an end. I made my last trip in July as the Air Corps program came to an end. This was also the end of my wartime experience. It had covered four-and-a-half years, a total of 66 Atlantic crossings with 4,300 flight hours covering about 300,000 miles. It was a very exciting time in my life.

I flew in three different uniforms — one civilian, one Navy, and one Army — and got to visit many cities and countries.

With the end of the war came the demise of the flying boats in transatlantic service. They were quickly sold off by Pan Am to be replaced by the much faster and economical DC-4s, which were converted military C-54s. The slow, costly flying boats quickly disappeared and all ceased to exist by 1950. It was a sad ending for a beautiful flying machine and for the nostalgic pilots who flew them.

Most of the flights came to be routine day-to-day work despite the imminent danger lurking in the background. There were special moments from time to time, however, and two stand out particularly in my memory.

The first occurred while I was still on commercial service. All co-pilots had to make a flight as a navigator training under the guidance of a professional navigator to qualify in flight navigation. On my trip one part was a westbound flight from West Africa across the South Atlantic to Natal, Brazil. It was a daylight crossing which meant we had to rely on dead reckoning using the wind direction and velocity, a less reliable method of navigation than celestial reckoning. To make it even more difficult, we were flying above a cloud deck which prevented good visibility of the ocean surface.

About 500 miles east of Natal is a rock formation that rises above the ocean, clearly visible from the air. According to my almost guess-work positioning, we were in that area. As I approached the cockpit to advise the pilots of the situation, I noticed a break in clouds ahead. With tongue in cheek in an attempt to break the tension, I said, "If you look down through the break ahead, you will see St. Paul's rocks." To the absolute amazement of everyone, especially me, there they were! The navigator told me that I had passed the test and that I could go to the passenger compartment and relax for the remainder of the trip.

The second event came on a Navy flight in the same area of Brazil. Flying from Natal to Belem, at the mouth of the Amazon River, the Captain told me he didn't feel well. He was able to land the plane but had to be hospitalized almost immediately. That left me in command of the plane and crew, as well as responsible for the passengers ... 23 sailors on their way home from the war.

I was advised that a replacement Captain would arrive in time for our scheduled takeoff the next morning. I knew our sailors were anxious to hit the local night clubs to celebrate. Before they left the terminal I gave them a lecture on what would happen to them if they missed the next morning's departure. A 23-year old civilian giving orders to 23 Navy veterans ... a most unusual situation and one I was not completely comfortable with.

Much to my surprise they all arrived at the terminal on time the following morning, although some had major hangovers. I imagine the fear of not getting home was great enough to overcome any distraction.

After everyone was on board I took my seat to await the arrival of our new Captain. After a short wait he arrived, announced that he was James Sommers, and took his place in the cockpit. I waited for an order and when it finally came it was a shock and a surprise. He turned to me and said, "Well, what are you waiting for? Take us home." It was a complete shock that someone who I had never flown with or even met face to face before would display so much confidence in me. After a short hesitation I proceeded to take off. We shared landings and takeoffs for the remainder of the trip. It was rare for any Captain to do that. At the end of the trip he arranged for me to be his regular co-pilot. Needless to say, it was the most memorable trip that I had ever made with Pan Am.

I flew as his First Officer on the remaining six trips in the Navy and continued to do so all through the eight flights in the Army Air Corps program. He was a very competent pilot with a background of flying in the Navy before coming to Pan Am. He was a pleasure to fly with, requiring only that each crew member performed his duty proficiently. Most of the Captains that I had flown with did not give their co-pilots many landings and takeoffs. Most had their own likes and dislikes. A few were not very pleasant to fly with. Sommers and I seemed to work well together and we became friends. It was always "Captain Sommers" and "Mister Young" while on duty, but less formal when we were off duty.

It was sad parting for me when the military flights came to an end and we each went our separate ways. Sommers resumed commercial flights to Europe out of the Atlantic Division, while I prepared for a transfer to the Latin American Division based in Miami.

In Miami I resumed my DC-3 training. Before long I started to make flights as a co-pilot on the reliable DC-3, the fourth plane in my Pan Am experience.

After three months I took my flight test to qualify as a command pilot. All went well and I started my career as a Captain flying to Havana and back to Miami, the easiest flight available. Soon I was flying to South and Central America on a regular basis. I did this steadily for four-and-a-half years.

At that point my father needed help in the family business. I decided to end my airline career and return to New York to join him. It was not an easy decision but it turned out to be the right one.

Born in Brooklyn, John grew up in Queens, N.Y. He graduated from Long Island University and after working as a pilot for Pan American Airlines, he was owner and president of J&A Young, Inc., a clothing manufacturer. He and his wife Louise had two children.

The War in Photos

Brownie McKinley poses with the harvest from her family's Victory Garden. Many households grew their own food to save resources for the troops on the front. Her story is found on Page 211.

For those waiting anxiously at home, letters were a lifeline to loved ones stationed far away. Warner Cornwall's war experiences are recounted in his letters home, found on Page 186.

Contributors

Andersen, George L. 166
Arthur, Bailey 173
Arthur, William C. 19
Bacon, Theodore S. 24
Bartlett, Sheppard 116
Blauner, Marcie 176
Britton, Jeanne McCutcheon 26
Brown, Mileva 177
Cahill, George F. Jr., M.D. 179
Chase, Robert A., M.D. 180
Clark, Barbara 183
Clinkenbeard, David 119
Collier, Judith E. 184
Cornwall, Warner B. 186
Crocker, Julie, M.D. 188
Faller, James 191
Fellows, Robert S. 30
Forman, Thomas H. 36
Goldsmith, Sharon H. 193
Goodhue, John 128
Goodnow, Molly 197
Goodnow, Sym 39
Gottschalk, Polly 199
Guion, Louise 41
Hewitt, Peter 130
Holcombe, Susanne 200
Isaac, René 43
Jacobs, Carl B. 132
Johnson, Robert D. 47
Keefe, John M. 52

Kelly, Christine S. 201
Kordalewski, Andrew 134
Lathrop, F.O. 60
Law, Augusta Foster, M.D. 203
Livingston, Helen W. 205
McClellan, Mary Elizabeth 208
McClellan, Bruce 62
Maynard, Doug 136
McKinley, Robert W. 211
Millard, Dr. Glyn 66
Moore, Harold C. Jr. 139
Moore, Irene Peacock 213
Morse, Birgit Faber 68
Nelson, Win 151
Oliver, Peter 73
Parker, Edith V. 218
Potter, Margo 219
Quick, Hazel S. 221
Sabine, G. Blake 77
Schmitt, Evelyn 227
Sherk, Donald M. 153
Sholl, Cal 155
Sholl, Nan 229
Stevenson, Arthur L. 160
Stoddard, Philip A. 81
Swahnberg, Richard 87
Van Strien, Karin 90
Walker, Sidney A. 232
Wilder, Alan 233
Wilson, Roger B. 99
Young, John J. 239

CPSIA information can be obtained at www.ICGtesting.com
Printed in the USA
BVOW010432210512

290466BV00005B/5/P